LEARN PYTHON 3
THE HARD WAY

Zed Shaw's Hard Way Series

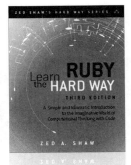

♦ Addison-Wesley

Visit **informit.com/hardway** for a complete list of available publications.

Zed Shaw's Hard Way Series emphasizes instruction and *making* things as the best way to get started in many computer science topics. Each book in the series is designed around short, understandable exercises that take you through a course of instruction that creates working software. All exercises are thoroughly tested to verify they work with real students, thus increasing your chance of success. The accompanying video walks you through the code in each exercise. Zed adds a bit of humor and inside jokes to make you laugh while you're learning.

Make sure to connect with us!
informit.com/socialconnect

LEARN PYTHON 3
THE HARD WAY

A Very Simple Introduction
to the Terrifyingly Beautiful World
of Computers and Code

Zed A. Shaw

✦▾ Addison-Wesley

Boston • Columbus • Indianapolis • New York • San Francisco • Amsterdam • Cape Town
Dubai • London • Madrid • Milan • Munich • Paris • Montreal • Toronto • Delhi • Mexico City
São Paulo • Sydney • Hong Kong • Seoul • Singapore • Taipei • Tokyo

Visit us on the Web: informit.com/aw

Library of Congress Control Number: 2017940290

ISBN-13: 978-0-13-469288-3
ISBN-10: 0-13-469288-8

3 18

Contents

Preface

This simple book is meant to get you started in programming. The title says it's the hard way to learn to write code, but it's actually not. It's only the "hard" way because it uses a technique called *instruction*. Instruction is where I tell you to do a sequence of controlled exercises designed to build a skill through repetition. This technique works very well with beginners who know nothing and need to acquire basic skills before they can understand more complex topics. It's used in everything from martial arts to music to even basic math and reading skills.

This book instructs you in Python by slowly building and establishing skills through techniques such as practice and memorization, then applying them to increasingly difficult problems. By the end of the book you will have the tools needed to begin learning more complex programming topics. I like to tell people that my book gives you your "programming black belt." What this means is that you know the basics well enough to now start learning programming.

If you work hard, take your time, and build these skills, you will learn to code.

Improvements in the Python 3 Edition

Learn Python 3 the Hard Way now uses Python 3.6. I've standardized on this version of Python because it has a new, improved string formatting system that is easier to use than the previous 4 (or 3, I forget, there were many) versions. There are a few problems with Python 3.6 for beginners, but I help you navigate these issues in the book. A particularly hairy problem is that Python 3.6 has very poor error messages in some key areas that I help you understand.

I have also improved the videos based on my experiences over the last five years teaching people Python. You can watch these videos online at informit.com/title/9780134692883. In the past the videos simply let you watch me do the exercise. The Python 3 edition videos also show you how to break—and then fix—every exercise. This skill is called "debugging." It teaches you how to fix problems you run into but also how Python runs the programs you're creating. The goal of this new methodology is to build a mental model of how Python runs your code so you can more easily figure out why it's broken. You'll also learn many useful tricks for debugging broken software.

Last, the Python 3 edition fully supports Microsoft Windows 10 from beginning to end. The previous edition focused mostly on the Unix-style systems such as macOS and Linux, with Windows being more of an afterthought. At the time I started writing the Python 3 edition Microsoft had started to take open source tools and developers seriously, and it was difficult to ignore them as a serious Python development platform. The videos feature Microsoft Windows using Python in various scenarios and also show macOS and Linux for full compatibility. I tell you about any gotchas on each platform, cover installation instructions, and provide any other tips I can give you.

The Hard Way Is Easier

With the help of this book, you will do the incredibly simple things that all programmers do to learn a programming language:

1.   Go through each exercise.

2.   Type in each file *exactly*.

3.   Make it run.

That's it. This will be *very* difficult at first, but stick with it. If you go through this book and do each exercise for one or two hours a night, you will have a good foundation for moving on to another book about Python to continue your studies. This book won't turn you into a programmer overnight, but it will get you started on the path to learning how to code.

This book's job is to teach you the three most essential skills that a beginning programmer needs to know: reading and writing, attention to detail, and spotting differences.

Reading and Writing

If you have a problem typing, you will have a problem learning to code, especially if you have a problem typing the fairly odd characters in source code. Without this simple skill you will be unable to learn even the most basic things about how software works.

Typing the code samples and getting them to run will help you learn the names of the symbols, get familiar with typing them, and get you reading the language.

Attention to Detail

The one skill that separates good programmers from bad programmers is attention to detail. In fact, it's what separates the good from the bad in any profession. You must pay attention to the tiniest details of your work or you will miss important elements of what you create. In programming, this is how you end up with bugs and difficult-to-use systems.

By going through this book, and copying each example *exactly*, you will be training your brain to focus on the details of what you are doing, as you are doing it.

Spotting Differences

A very important skill (that most programmers develop over time) is the ability to visually notice differences between things. An experienced programmer can take two pieces of code that are slightly different and immediately start pointing out the differences. Programmers have invented tools to make this even easier, but we won't be using any of these. You first have to train your brain the hard way, then use the tools.

While you do these exercises, typing each one in, you will make mistakes. It's inevitable; even seasoned programmers would make a few. Your job is to compare what you have written to what's required and fix all the differences. By doing so, you will train yourself to notice mistakes, bugs, and other problems.

Ask, Don't Stare

If you write code, you will write bugs. A "bug" means a defect, error, or problem with the code you've written. The legends say that this comes from an actual moth that flew into one of the first computers causing it to malfunction. Fixing it required "de-bugging" the computer. In the world of software, there are a *lot* of bugs. So many.

Like that first moth, your bugs will be hidden somewhere in the code, and you have to go find them. You can't just sit at your computer screen staring at the words you've written hoping that the answer jumps out at you. There is no more additional information you can get doing that, and you need additional information. You need to get up and go find the moth.

To do that you have to interrogate your code and ask it what is going on or look at the problem from a different view. In this book I frequently tell you to "stop staring and ask." I show you how to make your code tell you everything it can about what's going on and how to turn this into possible solutions. I also show you how to see your code in different ways, so you can get more information and insight.

Do Not Copy-Paste

You must *type* each of these exercises in, manually. If you copy-paste, you might as well not even do them. The point of these exercises is to train your hands, your brain, and your mind in how to read, write, and see code. If you copy-paste, you are cheating yourself out of the effectiveness of the lessons.

Using the Included Videos

Learn Python 3 the Hard Way has an extensive set of videos demonstrating how the code works and, most importantly, how to *break* it. The videos are the perfect place to demonstrate many common errors by breaking the Python code on purpose and showing you how to fix it. I also walk through the code using debugging and interrogation tricks and techniques. The videos are where I show you how to "stop staring and ask" the code what's wrong. You can watch these videos online at informit.com/title/9780134692883.

A Note on Practice and Persistence

While you are studying programming, I'm studying how to play guitar. I practice it every day for at least two hours a day. I play scales, chords, and arpeggios for an hour and then learn music theory, ear training, songs, and anything else I can. Some days I study guitar and music for eight hours because I feel like it and it's fun. To me repetitive practice is natural and just how to learn something. I know that to get good at anything I have to practice every day, even if I suck that day (which is often) or it's difficult. Keep trying, and eventually it'll be easier and fun.

Between the time that I wrote *Learn Python the Hard Way* and *Learn Ruby the Hard Way* I discovered drawing and painting. I fell in love with making visual art at the age of 39 and have been spending every day studying it in much the same way that I studied guitar, music, and programming. I collected books of instructional material, did what the books said, painted every day, and focused on enjoying the process of learning. I am by no means an "artist," or even that good, but I can now say that I can draw and paint. The same method I'm teaching you in this book applied to my adventures in art. If you break the problem down into small exercises and lessons, and do them every day, you can learn to do almost anything. If you focus on slowly improving and enjoying the learning process, then you will benefit no matter how good you are at it.

As you study this book, and continue with programming, remember that anything worth doing is difficult at first. Maybe you are the kind of person who is afraid of failure, so you give up at the first sign of difficulty. Maybe you never learned self-discipline, so you can't do anything that's "boring." Maybe you were told that you are "gifted," so you never attempt anything that might make you seem stupid or not a prodigy. Maybe you are competitive and unfairly compare yourself to someone like me who's been programming for more than 20 years.

Whatever your reason for wanting to quit, *keep at it*. Force yourself. If you run into a Study Drill you can't do, or a lesson you just do not understand, then skip it and come back to it later. Just keep going because with programming there's this very odd thing that happens. At first, you will not understand anything. It'll be weird, just like with learning any human language. You will struggle with words and not know what symbols are what, and it'll all be very confusing. Then, one day, *BANG*—your brain will snap and you will suddenly "get it." If you keep doing the exercises and keep trying to understand them, you will get it. You might not be a master coder, but you will at least understand how programming works.

If you give up, you won't ever reach this point. You will hit the first confusing thing (which is everything at first) and then stop. If you keep trying, keep typing it in, keep trying to understand it and reading about it, you will eventually get it. If you go through this whole book, and you still do not understand how to code, at least you gave it a shot. You can say you tried your best and a little more, and it didn't work out, but at least you tried. You can be proud of that.

> Register your copy of *Learn Python 3 the Hard Way* on the InformIT site for convenient access to updates and corrections as they become available. To start the registration process, go to informit.com/register and log in or create an account. Enter the product ISBN (9780134692883) and answer the simple proof-of-purchase question. Then look on the Registered Products tab for an Access Bonus Content link next to this product, and follow that link to access the bonus materials.

Acknowledgments

I would like to thank Angela for helping me with the first two versions of this book. Without her I probably wouldn't have bothered to finish it at all. She did the copyediting of the first draft and supported me immensely while I wrote it.

I'd also like to thank Greg Newman for doing the original cover art, Brian Shumate for early website designs, and all of the people who read this book and took the time to send me feedback and corrections.

Thank you.

The Setup

This exercise has no code. It is simply the exercise you complete to get your computer to run Python. You should follow these instructions as exactly as possible. If you have problems following the written instructions, then watch the included videos for your platform.

WARNING! If you do not know how to use PowerShell on Windows, Terminal on macOS or bash on Linux then you need to go learn that first. You should do the exercises in the appendix first before continuing with these exercises.

---

macOS

Do the following tasks to complete this exercise:

1. Go to https://www.python.org/downloads/release/python-360/ and download the version titled "Mac OS X 64-bit/32-bit installer." Install it like you would any other software.

2. Go to https://atom.io with your browser, get the Atom text editor, and install it. If Atom does not suit you, then see the *Alternative Text Editors* section at the end of this exercise.

3. Put Atom (your text editor) in your dock, so you can reach it easily.

4. Find your Terminal program. Search for it. You will find it.

5. Put your Terminal in your dock as well.

6. Run your Terminal program. It won't look like much.

7. In your Terminal program, run python3.6. You run things in Terminal by just typing the name and hitting RETURN.

8. Type quit(), Enter, and get out of python3.6.

9. You should be back at a prompt similar to what you had before you typed python. If not, find out why.

10. Learn how to make a directory in the Terminal.

11. Learn how to change into a directory in the Terminal.

12. Use your editor to create a file in this directory. Make the file, Save or Save As..., and pick this directory.

13.   Go back to Terminal using just the keyboard to switch windows.

14.   Back in Terminal, list the directory with ls to see your newly created file.

macOS: What You Should See

Here's me doing this on my macOS computer in Terminal. Your computer might be different but should be similar to this.

```
$ python3.6
Python 3.6.0 (default, Feb  2 2017, 12:48:29)
[GCC 4.2.1 Compatible Apple LLVM 7.0.2 (clang—700.1.81)] on darwin
Type "help", "copyright", "credits" or "license" for more information.
>>>
~ $ mkdir lpthw
~ $ cd lpthw
lpthw $ ls
# ... Use your text editor here to edit test.txt....
lpthw $ ls
test.txt
lpthw $
```

Windows

1.   Go to https://atom.io with your browser, get the Atom text editor, and install it. You do not need to be the administrator to do this.

2.   Make sure you can get to Atom easily by putting it on your desktop and/or in Quick Launch. Both options are available during setup. If you cannot run Atom because your computer is not fast enough, then see the *Alternative Text Editors* section at the end of this exercise.

3.   Run PowerShell from the Start menu. Search for it, and just press Enter to run it.

4.   Make a shortcut to it on your desktop and/or Quick Launch for your convenience.

5.   Run your PowerShell program (which I will call Terminal later). It won't look like much.

6.   Download Python 3.6 from https://www.python.org/downloads/release/python-360/ and install it. *Be sure to check the box that says to add Python 3.6 to your path.*

7.   In your PowerShell (Terminal) program, run python. You run things in Terminal by just typing the name and pressing Enter. If you type python and it does not run, then you have to reinstall Python and make sure you check the box for "Add python to the PATH." It's very small so look carefully.

8.   Type quit(), and press Enter to exit python.

9. You should be back at a prompt similar to what you had before you typed python. If not, find out why.

10. Learn how to make a directory in the PowerShell (Terminal).

11. Learn how to change into a directory in the PowerShell (Terminal).

12. Use your editor to create a file in this directory. Make the file, Save or Save As..., and pick this directory.

13. Go back to PowerShell (Terminal) using just the keyboard to switch windows. Look it up if you can't figure it out.

14. Back in PowerShell (Terminal), list the directory to see your newly created file.

From now on, when I say "Terminal" or "shell" I mean PowerShell, and that's what you should use. When I run python3.6 you can just type python.

Windows: What You Should See

```
> python
>>> quit()
> mkdir lpthw
> cd lpthw
... Here you would use your text editor to make test.txt in lpthw ...
>
> dir
 Volume in drive C is
 Volume Serial Number is 085C—7E02

 Directory of C:\Documents and Settings\you\lpthw

04.05.2010  23:32    <DIR>          .
04.05.2010  23:32    <DIR>          ..
04.05.2010  23:32                6 test.txt
               1 File(s)              6 bytes
               2 Dir(s)  14 804 623 360 bytes free


>
```

It is still correct if you see different information than mine, but yours should be similar.

Linux

Linux is a varied operating system with many different ways to install software. I'm assuming if you are running Linux then you know how to install packages, so here are your instructions:

1. Use your package manager to install Python 3.6, and if you can't, then download source from https://www.python.org/downloads/release/python-360/ and build from source.

2. Use your Linux package manager, and install the Atom text editor. If Atom does not suit you, then see the *Alternative Text Editors* section at the end of this exercise.

3. Make sure you can get to Atom easily by putting it in your window manager's menu.

4. Find your Terminal program. It could be called GNOME Terminal, Konsole, or xterm.

5. Put your Terminal in your dock as well.

6. Run your Terminal program. It won't look like much.

7. In your Terminal program, run python3.6. You run things in Terminal by just typing the command name and pressing Enter. If you can't run python3.6, try running just python.

8. Type quit() and press Enter to exit python.

9. You should be back at a prompt similar to what you had before you typed python. If not, find out why.

10. Learn how to make a directory in Terminal.

11. Learn how to change into a directory in Terminal.

12. Use your editor to create a file in this directory. Typically, you will make the file, Save or Save As..., and pick this directory.

13. Go back to Terminal using just the keyboard to switch windows. Look it up if you can't figure it out.

14. Back in Terminal, list the directory to see your newly created file.

Linux: What You Should See

```
$ python
>>> quit()
$ mkdir lpthw
$ cd lpthw
# ... Use your text editor here to edit test.txt ...
$ ls
test.txt
$
```

It is still correct if you see different information than mine, but yours should be similar.

Finding Things on the Internet

A major part of this book is learning to research programming topics online. I'll tell you to "search for this on the internet," and your job is to use a search engine to find the answer. The reason I have you search instead of just giving you the answer is because I want you to be an independent learner who does not need my book when you're done with it. If you can find the answers to your questions online, then you are one step closer to not needing me, and that is my goal.

Thanks to search engines such as Google you can easily find anything I tell you to find. If I say, "search online for the python list functions," then you simply do this:

1. Go to http://google.com.

2. Type: `python3 list functions`.

3. Read the websites listed to find the best answer.

Warnings for Beginners

You are done with this exercise. This exercise might be hard for you depending on your familiarity with your computer. If it is difficult, take the time to read and study and get through it, because until you can do these very basic things you will find it difficult to get much programming done.

If someone tells you to stop at a specific exercise in this book or to skip certain ones, you should ignore that person. Anyone trying to hide knowledge from you, or worse, make you get it from them instead of through your own efforts, is trying to make you depend on them for your skills. Don't listen to them, and do the exercises anyway so that you learn how to educate yourself.

A programmer will eventually tell you to use macOS or Linux. If the programmer likes fonts and typography, they'll tell you to get a macOS computer. If he likes control and has a huge beard, he will (or ze will if you prefer non-gendered pronouns for humans with beards) tell you to install Linux. Again, use whatever computer you have right now that works. All you need is an editor, a Terminal, and Python.

Finally, the purpose of this setup helps you do three things very reliably while you work on the exercises:

1. *Write* exercises using the text editor.

2. *Run* the exercises you wrote.

3. *Fix* them when they are broken.

4. Repeat.

Anything else will only confuse you, so stick to the plan.

Alternative Text Editors

Text editors are very important to a programmer, but as a beginner you only need a simple *programmer's text editor*. These are different from software for writing stories and books because they work with the unique needs of computer code. I recommend `Atom` in this book because it is free and works nearly everywhere. However, `Atom` may not run well on your computer, so here are some alternatives to try:

Editor Name	Works On	Where To Get It
Visual Studio Code	Windows, macOS, Linux	https://code.visualstudio.com
Notepad++	Windows	https://notepad-plus-plus.org
gEdit	Linux, macOS, Windows	https://github.com/GNOME/gedit
Textmate	macOS	https://github.com/textmate/textmate
SciTE	Windows, Linux	http://www.scintilla.org/SciTE.html
jEdit	Linux, macOS, Windows	http://www.jedit.org

These are ranked in order of most likely to work. Keep in mind that these projects may be abandoned, dead, or not work anymore on your computer. If you try one and it doesn't work, try another one. I've also listed the "Works On" in order of most likely to work, so if you're on Windows then look at the editors where Windows is listed first in the "Works On" column.

If you already know how to use Vim or Emacs then feel free to use them. If you have never used Vim or Emacs then avoid them. Programmers may try to convince you to use Vim or Emacs, but this will only derail you. Your focus is learning Python, not learning Vim or Emacs. If you try to use Vim and don't know how to quit, then type : q! or ZZ. If someone told you to use Vim, and they didn't even tell you this, then now you know why you shouldn't listen to them.

Do not use an Integrated Development Environment (IDE) while you go through this book. Relying on an IDE means that you can't work with new programming languages until some company decides to sell you an IDE for that language. This means you can't use that new language until the language is large enough to justify a lucrative customer base. If you are confident you can work with only a programmer's text editor (like Vim, Emacs, Atom, etc.) then you don't have to wait for a third party. IDEs are nice in some situations (such as working with a giant existing code base) but being addicted to them will limit your future.

You should also not use IDLE. It has serious limitations in how it works and isn't a very good piece of software. All you need is a simple text editor, a shell, and Python.

A Good First Program

WARNING! If you skipped Exercise 0, then you are not doing this book right. Are you trying to use IDLE or an IDE? I said not to use one in Exercise 0, so you should not use one. If you skipped Exercise 0 please go back to it and read it.

You should have spent a good amount of time in Exercise 0 learning how to install a text editor, run the text editor, run the Terminal, and work with both of them. If you haven't done that, then do not go on. You will not have a good time. This is the only time I'll start an exercise with a warning that you should not skip or get ahead of yourself.

Type the following text into a single file named ex1.py. Python works best with files ending in .py.

ex1.py

```
1    print("Hello World!")
2    print("Hello Again")
3    print("I like typing this.")
4    print("This is fun.")
5    print('Yay! Printing.')
6    print("I'd much rather you 'not'.")
7    print('I "said" do not touch this.')
```

Your Atom text editor should look something like this on all platforms:

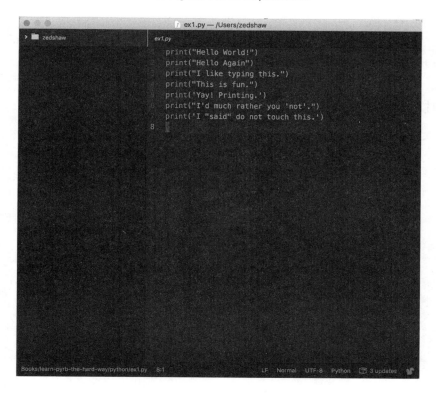

Don't worry if your editor doesn't look exactly the same; it should be close though. You may have a slightly different window header, maybe slightly different colors, and the left side of your Atom window won't say "zedshaw" but will instead show the directory you used for saving your files. All of those differences are fine.

When you create this file, keep in mind these points:

1. I did not type the line numbers on the left. Those are printed in the book so I can talk about specific lines by saying, "See line 5...." You do not type line numbers into Python scripts.

2. I have the `print` at the beginning of the line, and it looks exactly the same as what I have in `ex1.py`. Exactly means exactly, not kind of sort of the same. Every single character has to match for it to work. Color doesn't matter, only the characters you type.

In macOS Terminal or (maybe) Linux *run* the file by typing:

```
python3.6 ex1.py
```

On Windows, remember you *always* type `python` instead of `python3.6`, like this:

```
python ex1.py
```

If you did it right then you should see the same output as I in the *What You Should See* section of this exercise. If not, you have done something wrong. No, the computer is not wrong.

What You Should See

On macOS in the Terminal you should see this:

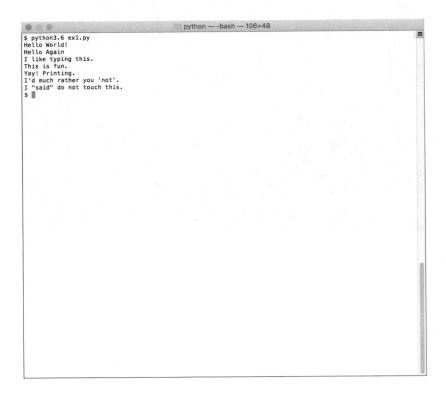

On Windows in PowerShell you should see this:

```
Windows PowerShell
PS C:\Users\zed\lpthw> python ex1.py
Hello World!
Hello Again
I like typing this.
This is fun.
Yay! Printing.
I'd much rather you 'not'.
I "said" do not touch this.
PS C:\Users\zed\lpthw>
```

You may see different names before the `python3.6 ex1.py` command, but the important part is that you type the command and see the output is the same as mine.

If you have an error it will look like this:

```
$ python3.6 python/ex1.py
  File "python/ex1.py", line 3
    print("I like typing this.
                              ^
SyntaxError: EOL while scanning string literal
```

It's important that you can read these error messages because you will be making many of these mistakes. Even I make many of these mistakes. Let's look at this line by line.

1. We ran our command in the Terminal to run the `ex1.py` script.

2. Python tells us that the file `ex1.py` has an error on line 3 of `ex1.py`.

3. It prints this line of code for us to see it.

4. Then it puts a ^ (caret) character to point at where the problem is. Notice the missing " (double-quote) character?

5. Finally, it prints out a "SyntaxError" and tells us something about what might be the error. Usually these are very cryptic, but if you copy that text into a search engine, you will find someone else's had that error, and you can probably figure out how to fix it.

Study Drills

The Study Drills contain things you should *try* to do. If you can't, skip it and come back later.

For this exercise, try these things:

1. Make your script print another line.

2. Make your script print only one of the lines.

3. Put a # (octothorpe) character at the beginning of a line. What did it do? Try to find out what this character does.

From now on, I won't explain how each exercise works unless an exercise is different.

WARNING! An "octothorpe" is also called a "pound," "hash," "mesh," or any number of other names. Pick the one that makes you chill out.

Common Student Questions

These are *actual* questions that real students have asked when doing this exercise.

Can I use IDLE?   No, you should use Terminal on macOS and PowerShell on Windows, just like I have here. If you don't know how to use those, then you can go read the appendix.

How do you get colors in your editor?   Save your file first as a `.py` file, such as `ex1.py`. Then you'll have color when you type.

I get `SyntaxError: invalid syntax` **when I run** `ex1.py.`   You are probably trying to run Python, then trying to type Python again. Close your Terminal, start it again, and right away type only `python3.6 ex1.py`.

I get `can't open file 'ex1.py': [Errno 2] No such file or directory.`   You need to be in the same directory as the file you created. Make sure you use the `cd` command to go there first. For example, if you saved your file in `lpthw/ex1.py`, then you would do `cd lpthw/` before trying to run `python3.6 ex1.py`. If you don't know what any of that means, then go through the appendix.

My file doesn't run; I just get the prompt back with no output.   You most likely took the code in my `ex1.py` file literally and thought that `print("Hello World!")` meant to type only `"Hello World!"` into the file, without the `print`. Your file has to be *exactly* like mine.

Comments and Pound Characters

Comments are very important in your programs. They are used to tell you what something does in English, and they are used to disable parts of your program if you need to remove them temporarily. Here's how you use comments in Python:

ex2.py

```
1    # A comment, this is so you can read your program later.
2    # Anything after the # is ignored by python.
3
4    print("I could have code like this.") # and the comment after is ignored
5
6    # You can also use a comment to "disable" or comment out code:
7    # print("This won't run.")
8
9    print("This will run.")
```

From now on, I'm going to write code like this. It is important for you to understand that everything does not have to be literal. Your screen and program may visually look different, but what's important is the text you type into the file you're writing in your text editor. In fact, I could work with any text editor and the results would be the same.

What You Should See

Exercise 2 Session

```
$ python3.6 ex2.py
I could have code like this.
This will run.
```

Again, I'm not going to show you screenshots of all the Terminals possible. You should understand that the preceding is not a literal translation of what your output should look like visually, but the text between the first $ python3.6 ... and last $ lines will be what you focus on.

Study Drills

1. Find out if you were right about what the # character does and make sure you know what it's called (octothorpe or pound character).

2. Take your ex2.py file and review each line going backward. Start at the last line, and check each word in reverse against what you should have typed.

3. Did you find more mistakes? Fix them.

4. Read what you typed above out loud, including saying each character by its name. Did you find more mistakes? Fix them.

Common Student Questions

Are you sure # is called the pound character?   I call it the octothorpe because that is the only name that no one country uses and that works in every country. Every country thinks its name for this one character is both the most important way to do it and the only way it's done. To me this is simply arrogance and, really, y'all should just chill out and focus on more important things like learning to code.

Why does the # in `print("Hi # there.")` **not get ignored?**   The # in that code is inside a string, so it will be put into the string until the ending " character is hit. Pound characters in strings are just considered characters, not comments.

How do I comment out multiple lines?   Put a # in front of each one.

I can't figure out how to type a # character on my country's keyboard. How do I do that?   Some countries use the ALT key and combinations of other keys to print characters foreign to their language. You'll have to look online in a search engine to see how to type it.

Why do I have to read code backward?   It's a trick to make your brain not attach meaning to each part of the code, and doing that makes you process each piece exactly. This is a handy error-checking technique.

Numbers and Math

Every programming language has some kind of way of doing numbers and math. Do not worry: programmers frequently lie about being math geniuses when they really aren't. If they were math geniuses, they would be doing math, not writing buggy web frameworks so they can drive race cars.

This exercise has lots of math symbols. Let's name them right away so you know what they are called. As you type this one in, say the name. When saying them feels boring you can stop saying them. Here are the names:

- +: plus
- -: minus
- /: slash
- *: asterisk
- %: percent
- <: less-than
- >: greater-than
- <=: less-than-equal
- >=: greater-than-equal

Notice how the operations are missing? After you type in the code for this exercise, go back and figure out what each of these does and complete the table. For example, + does addition.

ex3.py

```
 1    print("I will now count my chickens:")
 2
 3    print("Hens", 25 + 30 / 6)
 4    print("Roosters", 100 - 25 * 3 % 4)
 5
 6    print("Now I will count the eggs:")
 7
 8    print(3 + 2 + 1 - 5 + 4 % 2 - 1 / 4 + 6)
 9
10    print("Is it true that 3 + 2 < 5 - 7?")
11
12    print(3 + 2 < 5 - 7)
13
14    print("What is 3 + 2?", 3 + 2)
15    print("What is 5 - 7?", 5 - 7)
16
17    print("Oh, that's why it's False.")
```

```
18
19      print("How about some more.")
20
21      print("Is it greater?", 5 > -2)
22      print("Is it greater or equal?", 5 >= -2)
23      print("Is it less or equal?", 5 <= -2)
```

Make sure you type this exactly before you run it. Compare each line of your file to my file.

What You Should See

```
$ python3.6 ex3.py
I will now count my chickens:
Hens 30.0
Roosters 97
Now I will count the eggs:
6.75
Is it true that 3 + 2 < 5 - 7?
False
What is 3 + 2? 5
What is 5 - 7? -2
Oh, that's why it's False.
How about some more.
Is it greater? True
Is it greater or equal? True
Is it less or equal? False
```

Study Drills

1. Above each line, use the # to write a comment to yourself explaining what the line does.

2. Remember in Exercise 0 when you started python3.6? Start python3.6 this way again and, using the math operators, use Python as a calculator.

3. Find something you need to calculate and write a new .py file that does it.

4. Rewrite ex3.py to use floating point numbers so it's more accurate. 20.0 is floating point.

Common Student Questions

Why is the % character a "modulus" and not a "percent"?   Mostly that's just how the designers chose to use that symbol. In normal writing you are correct to read it as a "percent." In programming this calculation is typically done with simple division and the / operator. The % modulus is a different operation that just happens to use the % symbol.

How does % work?   Another way to say it is, "X divided by Y with J remaining." For example, "100 divided by 16 with 4 remaining." The result of % is the J part, or the remaining part.

What is the order of operations?   In the United States we use an acronym called PEMDAS which stands for Parentheses Exponents Multiplication Division Addition Subtraction. That's the order Python follows as well. The mistake people make with PEMDAS is to think this is a strict order, as in "Do P, then E, then M, then D, then A, then S." The actual order is you do the multiplication *and* division (M&D) in one step, from left to right, *then* you do the addition and subtraction in one step from left to right. So, you could rewrite PEMDAS as PE(M&D)(A&S).

Variables and Names

Now you can print things with `print` and you can do math. The next step is to learn about variables. In programming, a variable is nothing more than a name for something, similar to how my name, "Zed," is a name for "the human who wrote this book." Programmers use these variable names to make their code read more like English and because they have lousy memories. If they didn't use good names for things in their software, they'd get lost when they tried to read their code again.

If you get stuck with this exercise, remember the tricks you have been taught so far of finding differences and focusing on details:

1. Write a comment above each line explaining to yourself in English what it does.

2. Read your `.py` file backward.

3. Read your `.py` file out loud, saying even the characters.

ex4.py

```
1    cars = 100
2    space_in_a_car = 4.0
3    drivers = 30
4    passengers = 90
5    cars_not_driven = cars - drivers
6    cars_driven = drivers
7    carpool_capacity = cars_driven * space_in_a_car
8    average_passengers_per_car = passengers / cars_driven
9
10
11   print("There are", cars, "cars available.")
12   print("There are only", drivers, "drivers available.")
13   print("There will be", cars_not_driven, "empty cars today.")
14   print("We can transport", carpool_capacity, "people today.")
15   print("We have", passengers, "to carpool today.")
16   print("We need to put about", average_passengers_per_car,
17        "in each car.")
```

WARNING! The _ in `space_in_a_car` is called an *underscore character*. Find out how to type it if you do not already know. We use this character a lot to put an imaginary space between words in variable names.

What You Should See

```
$ python3.6 ex4.py
There are 100 cars available.
There are only 30 drivers available.
There will be 70 empty cars today.
We can transport 120.0 people today.
We have 90 to carpool today.
We need to put about 3.0 in each car.
```

Study Drills

When I wrote this program the first time I had a mistake, and Python told me about it like this:

```
Traceback (most recent call last):
  File "ex4.py", line 8, in <module>
    average_passengers_per_car = car_pool_capacity / passenger
NameError: name 'car_pool_capacity' is not defined
```

Explain this error in your own words. Make sure you use line numbers and explain why.

Here are more study drills:

1. I used 4.0 for `space_in_a_car`, but is that necessary? What happens if it's just 4?

2. Remember that 4.0 is a *floating point* number. It's just a number with a decimal point, and you need 4.0 instead of just 4 so that it is floating point.

3. Write comments above each of the variable assignments.

4. Make sure you know what = is called (equals) and that its purpose is to give data (numbers, strings, etc.) names (`cars_driven`, `passengers`).

5. Remember that _ is an underscore character.

6. Try running `python3.6` from the Terminal as a calculator like you did before, and use variable names to do your calculations. Popular variable names include `i`, `x`, and `j`.

Common Student Questions

What is the difference between = (single-equal) and == (double-equal)?   The = (single-equal) assigns the value on the right to a variable on the left. The == (double-equal) tests whether two things have the same value. You'll learn about this in Exercise 27.

Can we write x=100 **instead of** x = 100?   You can, but it's bad form. You should add space around operators like this so that it's easier to read.

What do you mean by "read the file backward"?   Very simple. Imagine you have a file with 16 lines of code in it. Start at line 16, and compare it to my file at line 16. Then do it again for 15, and so on until you've read the whole file backward.

Why did you use 4.0 **for** space_in_a_car?   It is mostly so you can then find out what a floating point number is and ask this question. See the Study Drills.

More Variables and Printing

N ow we'll do even more typing of variables and printing them out. This time we'll use something called a *format string*. Every time you put " (double-quotes) around a piece of text you have been making a *string*. A string is how you make something that your program might give to a human. You print strings, save strings to files, send strings to web servers, among many other things.

Strings are really handy, so in this exercise you will learn how to make strings that have variables embedded in them. You embed variables inside a string by using a special { } sequence and then put the variable you want inside the { } characters. You also must start the string with the letter f for "format," as in f"Hello {somevar}". This little f before the " (double-quote) and the { } characters tell Python 3, "Hey, this string needs to be formatted. Put these variables in there."

As usual, just type this in even if you do not understand it, and make it exactly the same.

ex5.py

```
1    my_name = 'Zed A. Shaw'
2    my_age = 35 # not a lie
3    my_height = 74 # inches
4    my_weight = 180 # lbs
5    my_eyes = 'Blue'
6    my_teeth = 'White'
7    my_hair = 'Brown'
8
9    print(f"Let's talk about {my_name}.")
10   print(f"He's {my_height} inches tall.")
11   print(f"He's {my_weight} pounds heavy.")
12   print("Actually that's not too heavy.")
13   print(f"He's got {my_eyes} eyes and {my_hair} hair.")
14   print(f"His teeth are usually {my_teeth} depending on the coffee.")
15
16   # this line is tricky, try to get it exactly right
17   total = my_age + my_height + my_weight
18   print(f"If I add {my_age}, {my_height}, and {my_weight} I get {total}.")
```

What You Should See

Exercise 5 Session

```
$ python3.6 ex5.py
Let's talk about Zed A. Shaw.
He's 74 inches tall.
```

```
He's 180 pounds heavy.
Actually that's not too heavy.
He's got Blue eyes and Brown hair.
His teeth are usually White depending on the coffee.
If I add 35, 74, and 180 I get 289.
```

Study Drills

1. Change all the variables so there is no my_ in front of each one. Make sure you change the name everywhere, not just where you used = to set them.

2. Try to write some variables that convert the inches and pounds to centimeters and kilograms. Do not just type in the measurements. Work out the math in Python.

Common Student Questions

Can I make a variable like this: `1 = 'Zed Shaw'`? No, 1 is not a valid variable name. They need to start with a character, so a1 would work, but 1 will not.

How can I round a floating point number? You can use the `round()` function like this: `round(1.7333)`.

Why does this not make sense to me? Try making the numbers in this script your measurements. It's weird, but talking about yourself will make it seem more real. Also, you're just starting out so it won't make too much sense. Keep going and more exercises will explain it more.

Strings and Text

While you have been writing strings, you still do not know what they do. In this exercise we create a bunch of variables with complex strings so you can see what they are for. First an explanation of strings.

A string is usually a bit of text you want to display to someone or "export" out of the program you are writing. Python knows you want something to be a string when you put either " (double-quotes) or ' (single-quotes) around the text. You saw this many times with your use of print when you put the text you want to go inside the string inside " or ' after the print to print the string.

Strings can contain any number of variables that are in your Python script. Remember that a variable is any line of code where you set a name = (equal) to a value. In the code for this exercise, types_of_people = 10 creates a variable named types_of_people and sets it = (equal) to 10. You can put that in any string with {types_of_people}. You also see that I have to use a special type of string to "format"; it's called an "f-string" and looks like this:

```
f"some stuff here {avariable}"
f"some other stuff {anothervar}"
```

Python *also* has another kind of formatting using the .format() syntax, which you see on line 17. You'll see me use that sometimes when I want to apply a format to an already-created string, such as in a loop. We'll cover that more later.

We will now type in a whole bunch of strings, variables, and formats, and print them. We will also practice using short, abbreviated variable names. Programmers love saving time at your expense by using annoyingly short and cryptic variable names, so let's get you started reading and writing them early on.

ex6.py

```
1   types_of_people = 10
2   x = f"There are {types_of_people} types of people."
3
4   binary = "binary"
5   do_not = "don't"
6   y = f"Those who know {binary} and those who {do_not}."
7
8   print(x)
9   print(y)
10
11  print(f"I said: {x}")
12  print(f"I also said: '{y}'")
13
14  hilarious = False
15  joke_evaluation = "Isn't that joke so funny?! {}"
16
```

```
17    print(joke_evaluation.format(hilarious))
18
19    w = "This is the left side of..."
20    e = "a string with a right side."
21
22    print(w + e)
```

What You Should See

```
$ python3.6 ex6.py
There are 10 types of people.
Those who know binary and those who don't.
I said: There are 10 types of people.
I also said: 'Those who know binary and those who don't.'
Isn't that joke so funny?! False
This is the left side of...a string with a right side.
```

Study Drills

1. Go through this program and write a comment above each line explaining it.

2. Find all the places where a string is put inside a string. There are four places.

3. Are you sure there are only four places? How do you know? Maybe I like lying.

4. Explain why adding the two strings w and e with + makes a longer string.

Break It

You are now at a point where you can try to break your code to see what happens. Think of this as a game to devise the most clever way to break the code. You can also find the simplest way to break it. Once you break the code, you then need to fix it. If you have a friend, then the two of you can try to break each other's code and fix it. Give your friend your ex6.py file so they can break something. Then you try to find their error and fix it. Have fun with this, and remember that if you wrote this code once you can do it again. If you take your damage too far, you can always type it in again for extra practice.

Common Student Questions

Why do you put ' (single-quotes) around some strings and not others?   Mostly it's because of style, but I'll use a single-quote inside a string that has double-quotes. Look at lines 6 and 15 to see how I'm doing that.

If you thought the joke was funny could you write hilarious = True?   Yes, and you'll learn more about these boolean values in Exercise 27.

More Printing

Now we are going to do a bunch of exercises where you just type code in and make it run. I won't be explaining this exercise because it is more of the same. The purpose is to build up your chops. See you in a few exercises, and *do not skip! Do not paste!*

ex7.py

```
1    print("Mary had a little lamb.")
2    print("Its fleece was white as {}.".format('snow'))
3    print("And everywhere that Mary went.")
4    print("." * 10)  # what'd that do?
5
6    end1 = "C"
7    end2 = "h"
8    end3 = "e"
9    end4 = "e"
10   end5 = "s"
11   end6 = "e"
12   end7 = "B"
13   end8 = "u"
14   end9 = "r"
15   end10 = "g"
16   end11 = "e"
17   end12 = "r"
18
19   # watch end = ' ' at the end. try removing it to see what happens
20   print(end1 + end2 + end3 + end4 + end5 + end6, end=' ')
21   print(end7 + end8 + end9 + end10 + end11 + end12)
```

What You Should See

Exercise 7 Session

```
$ python3.6 ex7.py
Mary had a little lamb.
Its fleece was white as snow.
And everywhere that Mary went.
..........
Cheese Burger
```

Study Drills

For these next few exercises, you will have the exact same Study Drills.

1. Go back through and write a comment on what each line does.

2. Read each one backward or out loud to find your errors.

3. From now on, when you make mistakes, write down on a piece of paper what kind of mistake you made.

4. When you go to the next exercise, look at the mistakes you have made and try not to make them in this new one.

5. Remember that everyone makes mistakes. Programmers are like magicians who fool everyone into thinking they are perfect and never wrong, but it's all an act. They make mistakes all the time.

Break It

Did you have fun breaking the code in Exercise 6? From now on you're going to break all the code you write or a friend's code. I won't have a *Break It* section explicitly in every exercise, but I will do this in almost every video. Your goal is to find as many different ways to break your code until you get tired or exhaust all possibilities. In some exercises I might point out a specific common way people break that exercise's code, but otherwise consider this a standing order to always break it.

Common Student Questions

Why are you using the variable named `'snow'`**?**   That's actually not a variable: it is just a string with the word snow in it. A variable wouldn't have the single-quotes around it.

Is it normal to write an English comment for every line of code like you say to do in Study Drill 1?   No, you write comments only to explain difficult-to-understand code or why you did something. Why is usually much more important, and then you try to write the code so that it explains how something is being done on its own. However, sometimes you have to write such nasty code to solve a problem that it does need a comment on every line. In this case it's strictly for you to practice translating code to English.

Can I use single-quotes or double-quotes to make a string or do they do different things?   In Python either way to make a string is acceptable, although typically you'll use single-quotes for any short strings like `'a'` or `'snow'`.

Printing, Printing

We will now see how to do a more complicated formatting of a string. This code looks complex, but if you do your comments above each line and break each thing down to its parts, you'll understand it.

ex8.py

```
1    formatter = "{} {} {} {}"
2
3    print(formatter.format(1, 2, 3, 4))
4    print(formatter.format("one", "two", "three", "four"))
5    print(formatter.format(True, False, False, True))
6    print(formatter.format(formatter, formatter, formatter, formatter))
7    print(formatter.format(
8        "Try your",
9        "Own text here",
10       "Maybe a poem",
11       "Or a song about fear"
12   ))
```

What You Should See

Exercise 8 Session

```
$ python3.6 ex8.py
1 2 3 4
one two three four
True False False True
{} {} {} {} {} {} {} {} {} {} {} {} {} {} {} {}
Try your Own text here Maybe a poem Or a song about fear
```

In this exercise I'm using something called a *function* to turn the formatter variable into other strings. When you see me write formatter.format(...) I'm telling python to do the following:

1. Take the formatter string defined on line 1.

2. Call its format function, which is similar to telling it to do a command line command named format.

3. Pass to format four arguments, which match up with the four {}s in the formatter variable. This is like passing arguments to the command line command format.

4. The result of calling format on formatter is a new string that has the {} replaced with the four variables. This is what print is now printing out.

That's a lot for the eighth exercise, so what I want you to do is consider this a brain teaser. It's alright if you don't *really* understand what's going on because the rest of the book will slowly make this clear. At this point, try to study this and see what's going on, then move on to the next exercise.

Study Drills

Do your checks, write down your mistakes, and try not to make the same mistakes on the next exercise. In other words, repeat the *Study Drills* from Exercise 7.

Common Student Questions

Why do I have to put quotes around `"one"` **but not around** `True` **or** `False`? Python recognizes `True` and `False` as keywords representing the concept of true and false. If you put quotes around them then they are turned into strings and won't work. You'll learn more about how these work in Exercise 27.

Can I use IDLE to run this? No, you should learn to use the command line. It is essential to learning programming and is a good place to start if you want to learn about programming. IDLE will fail for you when you get further in the book.

Printing, Printing, Printing

By now you should realize the pattern for this book is to use more than one exercise to teach you something new. I start with code that you might not understand, then more exercises explain the concept. If you don't understand something now, you will later as you complete more exercises. Write down what you don't understand, and keep going.

ex9.py

```
1    # Here's some new strange stuff, remember type it exactly.
2
3    days = "Mon Tue Wed Thu Fri Sat Sun"
4    months = "Jan\nFeb\nMar\nApr\nMay\nJun\nJul\nAug"
5
6    print("Here are the days: ", days)
7    print("Here are the months: ", months)
8
9    print("""
10   There's something going on here.
11   With the three double-quotes.
12   We'll be able to type as much as we like.
13   Even 4 lines if we want, or 5, or 6.
14   """)
```

What You Should See

Exercise 9 Session

```
$ python3.6 ex9.py
Here are the days:  Mon Tue Wed Thu Fri Sat Sun
Here are the months:  Jan
Feb
Mar
Apr
May
Jun
Jul
Aug

There's something going on here.
With the three double-quotes.
We'll be able to type as much as we like.
Even 4 lines if we want, or 5, or 6.
```

Study Drills

Check your work, write down your mistakes, try not to make them on the next exercise. Are you breaking your code and then fixing it? In other words, repeat the *Study Drills* from Exercise 7.

Common Student Questions

Why do I get an error when I put spaces between the three double-quotes?   You have to type them like `"""` and not `" " "`, meaning with *no* spaces between each one.

What if I wanted to start the months on a new line?   You simply start the string with \n, like this:

```
"\nJan\nFeb\nMar\nApr\nMay\nJun\nJul\nAug"
```

Is it bad that my errors are always spelling mistakes?   Most programming errors in the beginning (and even later) are simple spelling mistakes, typos, or getting simple things out of order.

What Was That?

In Exercise 9 I threw you some new stuff, just to keep you on your toes. I showed you two ways to make a string that goes across multiple lines. In the first way, I put the characters \n (backslash n) between the names of the months. These two characters put a *new line character* into the string at that point.

This \ (backslash) character encodes difficult-to-type characters into a string. There are various *escape sequences* available for different characters you might want to use. We'll try a few of these sequences so you can see what I mean.

An important escape sequence is to escape a single-quote (') or double-quote ("). Imagine you have a string that uses double-quotes and you want to put a double-quote inside the string. If you write "I "understand" joe." then Python will get confused because it will think the double-quotes around "understand" actually *ends* the string. You need a way to tell Python that the double-quote inside the string isn't a *real* double-quote.

To solve this problem you *escape* double-quotes and single-quotes so Python knows to include them in the string. Here's an example:

```
"I am 6'2\" tall."  # escape double-quote inside string
'I am 6\'2" tall.'  # escape single-quote inside string
```

The second way is by using triple-quotes, which is just """ and works like a string, but you also can put as many lines of text as you want until you type """ again. We'll also play with these.

ex10.py

```
1    tabby_cat = "\tI'm tabbed in."
2    persian_cat = "I'm split\non a line."
3    backslash_cat = "I'm \\ a \\ cat."
4
5    fat_cat = """
6    I'll do a list:
7    \t* Cat food
8    \t* Fishies
9    \t* Catnip\n\t* Grass
10   """
11
12   print(tabby_cat)
13   print(persian_cat)
14   print(backslash_cat)
15   print(fat_cat)
```

What You Should See

Look for the tab characters that you made. In this exercise the spacing is important to get right.

```
$ python ex10.py
        I'm tabbed in.
I'm split
on a line.
I'm \ a \ cat.

I'll do a list:
        * Cat food
        * Fishies
        * Catnip
        * Grass
```

Escape Sequences

This is all of the escape sequences Python supports. You may not use many of these, but memorize their format and what they do anyway. Try them out in some strings to see if you can make them work.

Escape	What it does.
\\	Backslash (\)
\'	Single-quote (')
\"	Double-quote (")
\a	ASCII bell (BEL)
\b	ASCII backspace (BS)
\f	ASCII formfeed (FF)
\n	ASCII linefeed (LF)
\N{name}	Character named name in the Unicode database (Unicode only)
\r	Carriage return (CR)
\t	Horizontal tab (TAB)
\uxxxx	Character with 16-bit hex value xxxx
\Uxxxxxxxx	Character with 32-bit hex value xxxxxxxx
\v	ASCII vertical tab (VT)
\000	Character with octal value 000
\xhh	Character with hex value hh

Study Drills

1.   Memorize all the escape sequences by putting them on flash cards.

2.   Use ' ' ' (triple-single-quote) instead. Can you see why you might use that instead of " " "?

3.   Combine escape sequences and format strings to create a more complex format.

Common Student Questions

I still haven't completely figured out the last exercise. Should I continue?   Yes, keep going. Instead of stopping, take notes listing things you don't understand for each exercise. Periodically go through your notes and see if you can figure these things out after you've completed more exercises. Sometimes, though, you may need to go back a few exercises and do them again.

What makes \\ special compared to the other ones?   It's simply the way you would write out one backslash (\) character. Think about why you would need this.

When I write // or /n it doesn't work.   That's because you are using a forward-slash (/) and not a backslash (\). They are different characters that do very different things.

I don't get Study Drill 3. What do you mean by "combine" escape sequences and formats?   One concept I need you to understand is that each of these exercises can be combined to solve problems. Take what you know about format strings and write some new code that uses format strings *and* the escape sequences from this exercise.

What's better, ' ' ' or " " "?   It's entirely based on style. Go with the ' ' ' (triple-single-quote) style for now, but be ready to use either depending on what feels best or what everyone else is doing.

Asking Questions

N ow it is time to pick up the pace. You are doing a lot of printing to get you familiar with typing simple things, but those simple things are fairly boring. What we want to do now is get data into your programs. This is a little tricky because you have to learn to do two things that may not make sense right away, but trust me and do it anyway. It will make sense in a few exercises.

Most of what software does is the following:

1. Takes some kind of input from a person.

2. Changes it.

3. Prints out something to show how it changed.

So far you have been printing strings, but you haven't been able to get any input from a person. You may not even know what "input" means, but type this code in anyway and make it exactly the same. In the next exercise we'll do more to explain input.

ex11.py

```
1   print("How old are you?", end=' ')
2   age = input()
3   print("How tall are you?", end=' ')
4   height = input()
5   print("How much do you weigh?", end=' ')
6   weight = input()
7
8   print(f"So, you're {age} old, {height} tall and {weight} heavy.")
```

WARNING! We put an end=' ' at the end of each print line. This tells print to not end the line with a newline character and go to the next line.

What You Should See

Exercise 11 Session

```
$ python3.6 ex11.py
How old are you? 38
How tall are you? 6'2"
How much do you weigh? 180lbs
So, you're 38 old, 6'2" tall and 180lbs heavy.
```

Study Drills

1. Go online and find out what Python's `input` does.

2. Can you find other ways to use it? Try some of the samples you find.

3. Write another "form" like this to ask some other questions.

Common Student Questions

How do I get a number from someone so I can do math? That's a little advanced, but try `x = int(input())`, which gets the number as a string from `input()`, then converts it to an integer using `int()`.

I put my height into raw input like this `input("6'2")` **but it doesn't work.** Don't put your height in there; type it directly into your Terminal. First, go back and make the code exactly like mine. Next, run the script, and when it pauses, type your height in at your keyboard. That's all there is to it.

Prompting People

When you typed input() you were typing the (and) characters, which are *parenthesis* characters. This is similar to when you used them to do a format with extra variables, as in f"{x} {y}". For input you can also put in a prompt to show to a person so he knows what to type. Put a string that you want for the prompt inside the () so that it looks like this:

```
y = input("Name? ")
```

This prompts the user with "Name?" and puts the result into the variable y. This is how you ask someone a question and get the answer.

This means we can completely rewrite our previous exercise using just input to do all the prompting.

ex12.py

```
1    age = input("How old are you? ")
2    height = input("How tall are you? ")
3    weight = input("How much do you weigh? ")
4
5    print(f"So, you're {age} old, {height} tall and {weight} heavy.")
```

What You Should See

Exercise 12 Session

```
$ python3.6 ex12.py
How old are you?  38
How tall are you?  6'2"
How much do you weigh?  180lbs
So, you're 38 old, 6'2" tall and 180lbs heavy.
```

Study Drills

1. In Terminal, where you normally run python3.6 to run your scripts, type pydoc input. Read what it says. If you're on Windows try python3.6 -m pydoc input instead.

2. Get out of pydoc by typing q to quit.

3. Look online for what the pydoc command does.

4. Use pydoc to also read about open, file, os, and sys. It's alright if you do not understand those; just read through and take notes about interesting things.

Common Student Questions

How come I get `SyntaxError: invalid syntax` **whenever I run** `pydoc`**?** You aren't running `pydoc` from the command line; you're probably running it from inside `python3.6`. Exit out of `python3.6` first.

Why does my `pydoc` **not pause like yours does?** Sometimes if the help document is short enough to fit on one screen then `pydoc` will just print it.

When I run `pydoc` **I get** `more is not recognized as an internal.` Some versions of Windows do not have that command, which means `pydoc` is broken for you. You can skip this Study Drill and just search online for Python documentation when you need it.

Why can't I do `print("How old are you?" , input())`**?** You can, but then the result of calling `input()` is never saved to a variable, and it'll work in a strange way. Try this, and then try to print out what you type. See if you can debug why this isn't working.

Parameters, Unpacking, Variables

I n this exercise we will cover one more input method you can use to pass variables to a script (*script* being another name for your .py files). You know how you type python3.6 ex13.py to run the ex13.py file? Well the ex13.py part of the command is called an *argument*. What we'll do now is write a script that also accepts arguments.

Type this program and I'll explain it in detail:

ex13.py

```
1    from sys import argv
2    # read the WYSS section for how to run this
3    script, first, second, third = argv
4
5    print("The script is called:", script)
6    print("Your first variable is:", first)
7    print("Your second variable is:", second)
8    print("Your third variable is:", third)
```

On line 1 we have what's called an *import*. This is how you add features to your script from the Python feature set. Rather than give you all the features at once, Python asks you to say what you plan to use. This keeps your programs small, but it also acts as documentation for other programmers who read your code later.

The argv is the *argument variable*, a very standard name in programming that you will find used in many other languages. This variable *holds* the arguments you pass to your Python script when you run it. In the exercises you will get to play with this more and see what happens.

Line 3 *unpacks* argv so that, rather than holding all the arguments, it gets assigned to four variables you can work with: script, first, second, and third. This may look strange, but "unpack" is probably the best word to describe what it does. It just says, "Take whatever is in argv, unpack it, and assign it to all of these variables on the left in order."

After that we just print them out like normal.

Hold Up! Features Have Another Name

I call them "features" here (these little things you import to make your Python program do more) but nobody else calls them features. I just used that name because I needed to trick you into learning what they are without jargon. Before you can continue, you need to learn their real name: *modules*.

From now on we will be calling these "features" that we `import` *modules*. I'll say things like, "You want to import the `sys` module." They are also called "libraries" by other programmers, but let's just stick with modules.

What You Should See

WARNING! Pay attention! You have been running python scripts without command line arguments. If you type only `python3.6 ex13.py` you are *doing it wrong!* Pay close attention to how I run it. This applies any time you see `argv` being used.

Run the program like this (and you *must* pass *three* command line arguments):

Exercise 13 Session

```
$ python3.6 ex13.py first 2nd 3rd
The script is called: ex13.py
Your first variable is: first
Your second variable is: 2nd
Your third variable is: 3rd
```

This is what you should see when you do a few different runs with different arguments:

Exercise 13 Session

```
$ python3.6 ex13.py stuff things that
The script is called: ex13.py
Your first variable is: stuff
Your second variable is: things
Your third variable is: that
$
$ python3.6 ex13.py apple orange grapefruit
The script is called: ex13.py
Your first variable is: apple
Your second variable is: orange
Your third variable is: grapefruit
```

You can actually replace `first`, 2nd, and 3rd with any three things you want.

If you do not run it correctly, then you will get an error like this:

Exercise 13 Session

```
$ python3.6 ex13.py first 2nd
Traceback (most recent call last):
  File "ex13.py", line 3, in <module>
    script, first, second, third = argv
ValueError: not enough values to unpack (expected 4, got 3)
```

This happens when you do not put enough arguments on the command when you run it (in this case just `first 2nd`). Notice that when I run it I give it `first 2nd`, which caused it to give an error about "need more than 3 values to unpack" telling you that you didn't give it enough parameters.

Study Drills

1. Try giving fewer than three arguments to your script. See that error you get? See if you can explain it.

2. Write a script that has fewer arguments and one that has more. Make sure you give the unpacked variables good names.

3. Combine `input` with `argv` to make a script that gets more input from a user. Don't overthink it. Just use `argv` to get something, and `input` to get something else from the user.

4. Remember that modules give you features. Modules. Modules. Remember this because we'll need it later.

Common Student Questions

When I run it I get `ValueError: need more than 1 value to unpack.` Remember that an important skill is paying attention to details. If you look at the *What You Should See* section you see that I run the script with parameters on the command line. You should replicate how I ran it exactly.

What's the difference between `argv` **and** `input()`? The difference has to do with where the user is required to give input. If they give your script inputs on the command line, then you use `argv`. If you want them to input using the keyboard while the script is running, then use `input()`.

Are the command line arguments strings? Yes, they come in as strings, even if you typed numbers on the command line. Use `int()` to convert them, like with `int(input())`.

How do you use the command line? You should have learned to use it very quickly and fluently by now, but if you need to learn it at this stage, then read the appendix.

I can't combine `argv` **with** `input()`. Don't overthink it. Just slap two lines at the end of this script that use `input()` to get something and then print it. From that, start playing with more ways to use both in the same script.

Why can't I do this: `input('? ') = x`? Because that's backward to how it should work. Do it the way I do it and it'll work.

Prompting and Passing

L et's do one exercise that uses argv and input together to ask the user something specific. You will need this for the next exercise where you learn to read and write files. In this exercise we'll use input slightly differently by having it print a simple > prompt. This is similar to games like *Zork* or *Adventure*.

ex14.py

```
1   from sys import argv
2
3   script, user_name = argv
4   prompt = '> '
5
6   print(f"Hi {user_name}, I'm the {script} script.")
7   print("I'd like to ask you a few questions.")
8   print(f"Do you like me {user_name}?")
9   likes = input(prompt)
10
11  print(f"Where do you live {user_name}?")
12  lives = input(prompt)
13
14  print("What kind of computer do you have?")
15  computer = input(prompt)
16
17  print(f"""
18  Alright, so you said {likes} about liking me.
19  You live in {lives}.  Not sure where that is.
20  And you have a {computer} computer.  Nice.
21  """)
```

We make a variable, prompt, that is set to the prompt we want, and we give that to input instead of typing it over and over. Now if we want to make the prompt something else, we just change it in this one spot and rerun the script. Very handy.

What You Should See

When you run this, remember that you have to give the script your name for the argv arguments.

Exercise 14 Session

```
$ python3.6 ex14.py zed
Hi zed, I'm the ex14.py script.
I'd like to ask you a few questions.
Do you like me zed?
>  Yes
```

```
Where do you live zed?
> San Francisco
What kind of computer do you have?
> Tandy 1000

Alright, so you said Yes about liking me.
You live in San Francisco.  Not sure where that is.
And you have a Tandy 1000 computer.  Nice.
```

Study Drills

1. Find out what the games *Zork* and *Adventure* were. Try to find copies and play them.

2. Change the `prompt` variable to something else entirely.

3. Add another argument and use it in your script, the same way you did in the previous exercise with `first, second = ARGV`.

4. Make sure you understand how I combined a `"""` style multiline string with the `{}` format activator as the last print.

Common Student Questions

I get `SyntaxError: invalid syntax` **when I run this script.**   Again, you have to run it right on the command line, not inside Python. If you type `python3.6`, and then try to type `python3.6 ex14.py Zed`, it will fail because you are running Python *inside* Python. Close your window and then just type `python3.6 ex14.py Zed`.

I don't understand what you mean by changing the prompt?   See the variable `prompt = '> '`. Change that to have a different value. You know this; it's just a string and you've done 13 exercises making them, so take the time to figure it out.

I get the error `ValueError: need more than 1 value to unpack`.   Remember when I said you need to look at the *What You Should See* section and replicate what I did? You need to do the same thing here, and focus on how I type the command in and why I have a command line argument.

How can I run this from IDLE?   Don't use IDLE.

Can I use double-quotes for the `prompt` **variable?**   You totally can. Go ahead and try that.

You have a Tandy computer?   I did when I was little.

I get `NameError: name 'prompt' is not defined` **when I run it.**   You either spelled the name of the `prompt` variable wrong or forgot that line. Go back and compare each line of code to mine, starting at the bottom of the script and working up to the top. Any time you see this error, it means you spelled something wrong or forgot to create the variable.

Reading Files

You know how to get input from a user with `input` or `argv`. Now you will learn about reading from a file. You may have to play with this exercise the most to understand what's going on, so do the exercise carefully and remember your checks. Working with files is an easy way to *erase your work* if you are not careful.

This exercise involves writing two files. One is the usual `ex15.py` file that you will run, but the *other* is named `ex15_sample.txt`. This second file isn't a script but a plain text file we'll be reading in our script. Here are the contents of that file:

```
This is stuff I typed into a file.
It is really cool stuff.
Lots and lots of fun to have in here.
```

What we want to do is *open* that file in our script and print it out. However, we do not want to just *hard code* the name `ex15_sample.txt` into our script. "Hard coding" means putting some bit of information that should come from the user as a string directly in our source code. That's bad because we want it to load other files later. The solution is to use `argv` or `input` to ask the user what file to open instead of hard coding the file's name.

ex15.py

```
1    from sys import argv
2
3    script, filename = argv
4
5    txt = open(filename)
6
7    print(f"Here's your file {filename}:")
8    print(txt.read())
9
10   print("Type the filename again:")
11   file_again = input("> ")
12
13   txt_again = open(file_again)
14
15   print(txt_again.read())
```

A few fancy things are going on in this file, so let's break it down real quickly:

- Lines 1–3 use `argv` to get a filename. Next we have line 5, where we use a new command, open. Right now, run `pydoc open` and read the instructions. Notice how, like your own scripts and `input`, it takes a parameter and returns a value you can set to your own variable. You just opened a file.

- Line 7 prints a little message, but on line 8 we have something very new and exciting. We call a function on `txt` named `read`. What you get back from `open` is a `file`, and it also has commands you can give it. You give a file a command by using the `.` (dot or period), the name of the command, and parameters, just like with `open` and `input`. The difference is that `txt.read()` says, "Hey `txt`! Do your read command with no parameters!"

The remainder of the file is more of the same, but we'll leave the analysis to you in the Study Drills.

What You Should See

WARNING! Pay attention! I said, *pay attention!* You have been running scripts with just the name of the script, but now that you are using `argv` you have to add arguments. Look at the very first line of the example below and you will see I do `python ex15.py ex15_sample.txt` to run it. See the extra argument `ex15_sample.txt` after the `ex15.py` script name. If you do not type that you will get an error, so *pay attention!*

I made a file called `ex15_sample.txt` and ran my script.

Exercise 15 Session

```
$ python3.6 ex15.py ex15_sample.txt
Here's your file ex15_sample.txt:
This is stuff I typed into a file.
It is really cool stuff.
Lots and lots of fun to have in here.


Type the filename again:
>  ex15_sample.txt
This is stuff I typed into a file.
It is really cool stuff.
Lots and lots of fun to have in here.
```

Study Drills

This is a big jump, so be sure you do this Study Drill as best you can before moving on.

1. Above each line, comment out in English what that line does.

2. If you are not sure, ask someone for help or search online. Many times searching for "python3.6 THING" will find answers to what that THING does in Python. Try searching for "python3.6 open."

3.   I used the word "commands" here, but commands are also called "functions" and "methods." You will learn about functions and methods later in the book.

4.   Get rid of lines 10–15 where you use `input` and run the script again.

5.   Use only `input` and try the script that way. Why is one way of getting the filename better than another?

6.   Start `python3.6` to start the `python3.6` shell, and use `open` from the prompt just like in this program. Notice how you can open files and run `read` on them from within `python3.6`?

7.   Have your script also call `close()` on the `txt` and `txt_again` variables. It's important to close files when you are done with them.

Common Student Questions

Does `txt = open(filename)` return the contents of the file?   No, it doesn't. It actually makes something called a *file object*. You can think of a file like an old tape drive that you saw on mainframe computers in the 1950s or even like a DVD player from today. You can move around inside them and then "read" them, but the DVD player is not the DVD the same way the file object is not the file's contents.

I can't type code into Terminal/PowerShell like you say in Study Drill 7.   First, from the command line just type `python3.6` and press Enter. Now you are in `python3.6` as we've done a few other times. Then you can type in code and Python will run it in little pieces. Play with that. To get out of it type `quit()` and hit Enter.

Why is there no error when we open the file twice?   Python will not restrict you from opening a file more than once, and sometimes this is necessary.

What does `from sys import argv` mean?   For now just understand that `sys` is a package, and this phrase just says to get the `argv` feature from that package. You'll learn more about these later.

I put the name of the file in as `script, ex15_sample.txt = argv`, but it doesn't work.   No, that's not how you do it. Make the code exactly like mine, then run it from the command line the exact same way I do. You don't put the names of files in, you let Python put the name in.

EXERCISE 16

Reading and Writing Files

If you did the Study Drills from the last exercise, you should have seen all sorts of commands (methods/functions) you can give to files. Here's the list of commands I want you to remember:

- `close`: Closes the file. Like `File->Save...` in your editor.
- `read`: Reads the contents of the file. You can assign the result to a variable.
- `readline`: Reads just one line of a text file.
- `truncate`: Empties the file. Watch out if you care about the file.
- `write('stuff')`: Writes "stuff" to the file.
- `seek(0)`: Moves the read/write location to the beginning of the file.

One way to remember what each of these does is to think of a vinyl record, cassette tape, VHS tape, DVD, or CD player. In the early days of computers, data was stored on each of these kinds of media, so many of the file operations still resemble a storage system that is linear. Tape and DVD drives need to "seek" a specific spot, and then you can read or write at that spot. Today we have operating systems and storage media that blur the lines between random access memory and disk drives, but we still use the older idea of a linear tape with a read/write head that must be moved.

For now, these are the important commands you need to know. Some of them take parameters, but we do not really care about that. You only need to remember that `write` takes a parameter of a string you want to write to the file.

Let's use some of this to make a simple little text editor:

ex16.py

```
1    from sys import argv
2
3    script, filename = argv
4
5    print(f"We're going to erase {filename}.")
6    print("If you don't want that, hit CTRL-C (^C).")
7    print("If you do want that, hit RETURN.")
8
9    input("?")
10
11   print("Opening the file...")
12   target = open(filename, 'w')
13
14   print("Truncating the file.  Goodbye!")
15   target.truncate()
16
17   print("Now I'm going to ask you for three lines.")
```

```
18
19    line1 = input("line 1: ")
20    line2 = input("line 2: ")
21    line3 = input("line 3: ")
22
23    print("I'm going to write these to the file.")
24
25    target.write(line1)
26    target.write("\n")
27    target.write(line2)
28    target.write("\n")
29    target.write(line3)
30    target.write("\n")
31
32    print("And finally, we close it.")
33    target.close()
```

That's a large file, probably the largest you have typed in. So go slow, do your checks, and make it run. One trick is to get bits of it running at a time. Get lines 1–8 running, then five more, then a few more, until it's all done and running.

What You Should See

There are actually two things you will see. First, the output of your new script:

Exercise 16 Session

```
$ python3.6 ex16.py test.txt
We're going to erase test.txt.
If you don't want that, hit CTRL-C (^C).
If you do want that, hit RETURN.
?
Opening the file...
Truncating the file.  Goodbye!
Now I'm going to ask you for three lines.
line 1:  Mary had a little lamb
line 2:  Its fleece was white as snow
line 3:  It was also tasty
I'm going to write these to the file.
And finally, we close it.
```

Now, open up the file you made (in my case, test.txt) in your editor and check it out. Neat, right?

Study Drills

1. If you do not understand this, go back through and use the comment trick to get it squared away in your mind. One simple English comment above each line will help you understand or at least let you know what you need to research more.

2. Write a script similar to the last exercise that uses `read` and `argv` to read the file you just created.

3. There's too much repetition in this file. Use strings, formats, and escapes to print out `line1`, `line2`, and `line3` with just one `target.write()` command instead of six.

4. Find out why we had to pass a `'w'` as an extra parameter to `open`. Hint: open tries to be safe by making you explicitly say you want to write a file.

5. If you open the file with `'w'` mode, then do you really need the `target.truncate()`? Read the documentation for Python's open function and see if that's true.

Common Student Questions

Is the `truncate()` necessary with the `'w'` parameter?   See Study Drills number 5.

What does `'w'` mean?   It's really just a string with a character in it for the kind of mode for the file. If you use `'w'` then you're saying "open this file in 'write' mode," thus the `'w'` character. There's also `'r'` for "read," `'a'` for "append," and modifiers on these.

What modifiers to the file modes can I use?   The most important one to know for now is the + modifier, so you can do `'w+'`, `'r+'`, and `'a+'`. This will open the file in both read and write mode and, depending on the character use, position the file in different ways.

Does just doing open(filename) **open it in** `'r'` **(read) mode?**   Yes, that's the default for the open() function.

More Files

N ow let's do a few more things with files. We'll write a Python script to copy one file to another. It'll be very short but will give you ideas about other things you can do with files.

ex17.py

```
1    from sys import argv
2    from os.path import exists
3
4    script, from_file, to_file = argv
5
6    print(f"Copying from {from_file} to {to_file}")
7
8    # we could do these two on one line, how?
9    in_file = open(from_file)
10   indata = in_file.read()
11
12   print(f"The input file is {len(indata)} bytes long")
13
14   print(f"Does the output file exist? {exists(to_file)}")
15   print("Ready, hit RETURN to continue, CTRL-C to abort.")
16   input()
17
18   out_file = open(to_file, 'w')
19   out_file.write(indata)
20
21   print("Alright, all done.")
22
23   out_file.close()
24   in_file.close()
```

You should immediately notice that we import another handy command named exists. This returns True if a file exists, based on its name in a string as an argument. It returns False if not. We'll be using this function in the second half of this book to do lots of things, but right now you should see how you can import it.

Using import is a way to get tons of free code other better (well, usually) programmers have written so you do not have to write it.

What You Should See

Just like your other scripts, run this one with two arguments: the file to copy from and the file to copy it to. I'm going to use a simple test file named test.txt:

```
$ # first make a sample file
$ echo "This is a test file." > test.txt
$ # then look at it
$ cat test.txt
This is a test file.
$ # now run our script on it
$ python3.6 ex17.py test.txt new_file.txt
Copying from test.txt to new_file.txt
The input file is 21 bytes long
Does the output file exist? False
Ready, hit RETURN to continue, CTRL-C to abort.

Alright, all done.
```

It should work with any file. Try a bunch more and see what happens. Just be careful you do not blast an important file.

WARNING! Did you see the trick I did with echo to make a file and cat to show the file? You can learn how to do that in the Appendix, "Command Line Crash Course."

Study Drills

1. This script is *really* annoying. There's no need to ask you before doing the copy, and it prints too much out to the screen. Try to make the script more friendly to use by removing features.

2. See how short you can make the script. I could make this one line long.

3. Notice at the end of the *What You Should See* section I used something called cat? It's an old command that con*cat*enates files together, but mostly it's just an easy way to print a file to the screen. Type man cat to read about it.

4. Find out why you had to write out_file.close() in the code.

5. Go read up on Python's import statement, and start python3.6 to try it out. Try importing some things and see if you can get it right. It's alright if you do not.

Common Student Questions

Why is the 'w' in quotes? That's a string. You've been using strings for a while now. Make sure you know what a string is.

No way you can make this one line! That ; depends ; on ; how ; you ; define ; one ; line ; of ; code.

Is it normal to feel like this exercise was really hard? Yes, it is totally normal. Programming may not "click" for you until maybe even Exercise 36, or it might not until you finish the book and then make something with Python. Everyone is different, so just keep going and keep reviewing exercises that you had trouble with until it clicks. Be patient.

What does the `len()` function do? It gets the length of the string that you pass to it then returns that as a number. Play with it.

When I try to make this script shorter I get an error when I close the files at the end. You probably did something like `indata = open(from_file).read()`, which means you don't need to then do `in_file.close()` when you reach the end of the script. It should already be closed by Python once that one line runs.

I get a `Syntax:EOL while scanning string literal` error. You forgot to end a string properly with a quote. Go look at that line again.

Names, Variables, Code, Functions

B ig title, right? I am about to introduce you to *the function!* Dum dum dah! Every programmer will go on and on about functions and all the different ideas about how they work and what they do, but I will give you the simplest explanation you can use right now.

Functions do three things:

1. They name pieces of code the way variables name strings and numbers.

2. They take arguments the way your scripts take argv.

3. Using 1 and 2, they let you make your own "mini-scripts" or "tiny commands."

You can create a function by using the word def in Python. I'm going to have you make four different functions that work like your scripts, and then I'll show you how each one is related.

ex18.py

```
1     # this one is like your scripts with argv
2     def print_two(*args):
3         arg1, arg2 = args
4         print(f"arg1: {arg1}, arg2: {arg2}")
5
6     # ok, that *args is actually pointless, we can just do this
7     def print_two_again(arg1, arg2):
8         print(f"arg1: {arg1}, arg2: {arg2}")
9
10    # this just takes one argument
11    def print_one(arg1):
12        print(f"arg1: {arg1}")
13
14    # this one takes no arguments
15    def print_none():
16        print("I got nothin'.")
17
18
19    print_two("Zed","Shaw")
20    print_two_again("Zed","Shaw")
21    print_one("First!")
22    print_none()
```

Let's break down the first function, print_two, which is the most similar to what you already know from making scripts:

1. We tell Python we want to make a function using def for "define."

2. On the same line as def we give the function a name. In this case we just called it "print_two," but it could also be "peanuts." It doesn't matter, except that your function should have a short name that says what it does.

3. We tell it we want *args (asterisk args), which is a lot like your argv parameter but for functions. This *has* to go inside parentheses to work.

4. We end this line with a : (colon) and start indenting.

5. After the colon, all the lines that are indented four spaces will become attached to print_two. Our first indented line is one that unpacks the arguments, the same as with your scripts.

6. To demonstrate how it works we print these arguments out, just like we would in a script.

The problem with print_two is that it's not the easiest way to make a function. In Python we can skip the whole unpacking arguments and just use the names we want right inside parentheses. That's what print_two_again does.

After that you have an example of how you make a function that takes one argument in print_one.

Finally you have a function that has no arguments in print_none.

WARNING! This is very important. Do *not* get discouraged right now if this doesn't quite make sense. We're going to do a few exercises linking functions to your scripts and show you how to make more. For now, just keep thinking "mini-script" when I say "function" and keep playing with them.

What You Should See

If you run ex18.py you should see:

Exercise 18 Session

```
$ python3.6 ex18.py
arg1: Zed, arg2: Shaw
arg1: Zed, arg2: Shaw
arg1: First!
I got nothin'.
```

Right away you can see how a function works. Notice that you used your functions the way you use things like exists, open, and other commands. In fact, I've been tricking you because in Python those commands are just functions. This means you can make your own commands and use them in your scripts, too.

Study Drills

Create a *function checklist* for later exercises. Write these checks on an index card and keep it by you while you complete the rest of these exercises or until you feel you do not need the index card anymore:

1. Did you start your function definition with `def`?
2. Does your function name have only characters and _ (underscore) characters?
3. Did you put an open parenthesis right after the function name?
4. Did you put your arguments after the parenthesis separated by commas?
5. Did you make each argument unique (meaning no duplicated names)?
6. Did you put a close parenthesis and a colon after the arguments?
7. Did you indent all lines of code you want in the function four spaces? No more, no less.
8. Did you "end" your function by going back to writing with no indent (*dedenting*, we call it)?

When you run ("use" or "call") a function, check these things:

1. Did you call/use/run this function by typing its name?
2. Did you put the (character after the name to run it?
3. Did you put the values you want into the parentheses separated by commas?
4. Did you end the function call with a) character?

Use these two checklists on the remaining lessons until you do not need them anymore.

Finally, repeat this a few times to yourself: To "run," "call," or "use" a function each means the same thing.

Common Student Questions

What's allowed for a function name?   The same as variable names. Anything that doesn't start with a number and is letters, numbers, and underscores will work.

What does the * in `*args` do?   That tells Python to take all the arguments to the function and then put them in `args` as a list. It's like `argv` that you've been using but for functions. It's not normally used too often unless specifically needed.

This feels really boring and monotonous.   That's good. It means you're starting to get better at typing in the code and understanding what it does. To make it less boring, take everything I tell you to type in, and then break it on purpose.

Functions and Variables

Functions may have been a mind-blowing amount of information, but do not worry. Just keep doing these exercises and going through your checklist from the last exercise and you will eventually get it.

There is one tiny point that you might not have realized, which we'll reinforce right now. The variables in your function are not connected to the variables in your script. Here's an exercise to get you thinking about this:

ex19.py

```
1    def cheese_and_crackers(cheese_count, boxes_of_crackers):
2        print(f"You have {cheese_count} cheeses!")
3        print(f"You have {boxes_of_crackers} boxes of crackers!")
4        print("Man that's enough for a party!")
5        print("Get a blanket.\n")
6
7
8    print("We can just give the function numbers directly:")
9    cheese_and_crackers(20, 30)
10
11
12   print("OR, we can use variables from our script:")
13   amount_of_cheese = 10
14   amount_of_crackers = 50
15
16   cheese_and_crackers(amount_of_cheese, amount_of_crackers)
17
18
19   print("We can even do math inside too:")
20   cheese_and_crackers(10 + 20, 5 + 6)
21
22
23   print("And we can combine the two, variables and math:")
24   cheese_and_crackers(amount_of_cheese + 100, amount_of_crackers + 1000)
```

This shows all the different ways we're able to give our function cheese_and_crackers the values it needs to print them. We can give it straight numbers. We can give it variables. We can give it math. We can even combine math and variables.

In a way, the arguments to a function are kind of like our = character when we make a variable. In fact, if you can use = to name something, you can usually pass it to a function as an argument.

What You Should See

You should study the output of this script and compare it with what you think you should get for each of the examples in the script.

```
$ python3.6 ex19.py
We can just give the function numbers directly:
You have 20 cheeses!
You have 30 boxes of crackers!
Man that's enough for a party!
Get a blanket.

OR, we can use variables from our script:
You have 10 cheeses!
You have 50 boxes of crackers!
Man that's enough for a party!
Get a blanket.

We can even do math inside too:
You have 30 cheeses!
You have 11 boxes of crackers!
Man that's enough for a party!
Get a blanket.

And we can combine the two, variables and math:
You have 110 cheeses!
You have 1050 boxes of crackers!
Man that's enough for a party!
Get a blanket.
```

Study Drills

1. Go back through the script and type a comment above each line explaining in English what it does.

2. Start at the bottom and read each line backward, saying all the important characters.

3. Write at least one more function of your own design, and run it 10 different ways.

Common Student Questions

How can there possibly be 10 different ways to run a function? Believe it or not, there's a theoretically infinite number of ways to call any function. See how creative you can get with functions, variables, and input from a user.

Is there a way to analyze what this function is doing so I can understand it better? There are many different ways, but try putting an English comment above each line describing what the line does. Another trick is to read the code out loud. Yet another is to print the code out and draw on the paper with pictures and comments showing what's going on.

What if I want to ask the user for the numbers of cheese and crackers? You need to use `int()` to convert what you get from `input()`.

Does making the variable `amount_of_cheese` change the variable `cheese_count` in the function? No, those variables are separate and live outside the function. They are then passed to the function, and temporary versions are made just for the function's run. When the function exits, these temporary variables go away and everything keeps working. Keep going in the book, and this should become clearer.

Is it bad to have global variables (like `amount_of_cheese`) with the same name as function variables? Yes, since then you're not quite sure which one you're talking about. But sometimes necessity means you have to use the same name, or you might do it on accident. Just avoid it whenever you can.

Is there a limit to the number of arguments a function can have? It depends on the version of Python and the computer you're on, but it is fairly large. The practical limit though is about five arguments before the function becomes annoying to use.

Can you call a function within a function? Yes, you'll make a game that does this later in the book.

Functions and Files

Remember your checklist for functions, then do this exercise paying close attention to how functions and files can work together to make useful stuff.

ex20.py

```python
from sys import argv

script, input_file = argv

def print_all(f):
    print(f.read())

def rewind(f):
    f.seek(0)

def print_a_line(line_count, f):
    print(line_count, f.readline())

current_file = open(input_file)

print("First let's print the whole file:\n")

print_all(current_file)

print("Now let's rewind, kind of like a tape.")

rewind(current_file)

print("Let's print three lines:")

current_line = 1
print_a_line(current_line, current_file)

current_line = current_line + 1
print_a_line(current_line, current_file)

current_line = current_line + 1
print_a_line(current_line, current_file)
```

Pay close attention to how we pass in the current line number each time we run `print_a_line`.

What You Should See

```
$ python3.6 ex20.py test.txt
First let's print the whole file:

This is line 1
This is line 2
This is line 3

Now let's rewind, kind of like a tape.
Let's print three lines:
1 This is line 1

2 This is line 2

3 This is line 3
```

Study Drills

1. Write an English comment for each line to understand what that line does.
2. Each time `print_a_line` is run, you are passing in a variable, `current_line`. Write out what `current_line` is equal to on each function call, and trace how it becomes `line_count` in `print_a_line`.
3. Find each place a function is used, and check its `def` to make sure that you are giving it the right arguments.
4. Research online what the `seek` function for `file` does. Try `pydoc file`, and see if you can figure it out from there. Then try `pydoc file.seek` to see what seek does.
5. Research the shorthand notation `+=`, and rewrite the script to use `+=` instead.

Common Student Questions

What is `f` **in the** `print_all` **and other functions?**   The `f` is a variable just like you had in other functions in Exercise 18, except this time it's a file. A file in Python is kind of like an old tape drive on a mainframe or maybe a DVD player. It has a "read head," and you can "seek" this read head around the file to positions, then work with it there. Each time you do `f.seek(0)` you're moving to the start of the file. Each time you do `f.readline()` you're reading a line from the file and moving the read head to right after the `\n` that ends that line. This will be explained more as you go on.

Why does `seek(0)` **not set the** `current_line` **to 0?**   First, the `seek()` function is dealing in *bytes*, not lines. The code `seek(0)` moves the file to the 0 byte (first byte) in the file. Second, `current_line` is just a variable and has no real connection to the file at all. We are manually incrementing it.

What is +=?   You know how in English I can rewrite "it is" as "it's"? Or I can rewrite "you are" as "you're"? In English this is called a contraction, and this is kind of like a contraction for the two operations = and +. That means `x = x + y` is the same as `x += y`.

How does `readline()` **know where each line is?**   Inside `readline()` is code that scans each byte of the file until it finds a \n character, then stops reading the file to return what it found so far. The file `f` is responsible for maintaining the current position in the file after each `readline()` call, so that it will keep reading each line.

Why are there empty lines between the lines in the file?   The `readline()` function returns the \n that's in the file at the end of that line. Add a `end = ""` at the end of your `print` function calls to avoid adding double \n to every line.

Functions Can Return Something

You have been using the = character to name variables and set them to numbers or strings. We're now going to blow your mind again by showing you how to use = and a new Python word, `return`, to set variables to be a *value from a function*. There will be one thing to pay close attention to, but first type this in:

ex21.py

```python
def add(a, b):
    print(f"ADDING {a} + {b}")
    return a + b

def subtract(a, b):
    print(f"SUBTRACTING {a} - {b}")
    return a - b

def multiply(a, b):
    print(f"MULTIPLYING {a} * {b}")
    return a * b

def divide(a, b):
    print(f"DIVIDING {a} / {b}")
    return a / b


print("Let's do some math with just functions!")

age = add(30, 5)
height = subtract(78, 4)
weight = multiply(90, 2)
iq = divide(100, 2)

print(f"Age: {age}, Height: {height}, Weight: {weight}, IQ: {iq}")


# A puzzle for the extra credit, type it in anyway.
print("Here is a puzzle.")

what = add(age, subtract(height, multiply(weight, divide(iq, 2))))

print("That becomes: ", what, "Can you do it by hand?")
```

We are now doing our own math functions for `add`, `subtract`, `multiply`, and `divide`. The important thing to notice is the last line where we say `return a + b` (in add). What this does is the following:

1. Our function is called with two arguments: a and b.

2. We print out what our function is doing, in this case "ADDING."

3. We tell Python to do something kind of backward: we return the addition of a + b. You might say this as, "I add a and b, then return them."

4. Python adds the two numbers. Then when the function ends, any line that runs it will be able to assign this a + b result to a variable.

As with many other things in this book, you should take this real slow, break it down, and try to trace what's going on. To help there is extra credit to solve a puzzle and learn something cool.

What You Should See

Exercise 21 Session

```
$ python3.6 ex21.py
Let's do some math with just functions!
ADDING 30 + 5
SUBTRACTING 78 - 4
MULTIPLYING 90 * 2
DIVIDING 100 / 2
Age: 35, Height: 74, Weight: 180, IQ: 50.0
Here is a puzzle.
DIVIDING 50.0 / 2
MULTIPLYING 180 * 25.0
SUBTRACTING 74 - 4500.0
ADDING 35 + -4426.0
That becomes:  -4391.0 Can you do it by hand?
```

Study Drills

1. If you aren't really sure what `return` does, try writing a few of your own functions and have them return some values. You can return anything that you can put to the right of an =.

2. At the end of the script is a puzzle. I'm taking the return value of one function and *using* it as the argument of another function. I'm doing this in a chain so that I'm kind of creating a formula using the functions. It looks really weird, but if you run the script, you can see the results. What you should do is try to figure out the normal formula that would recreate this same set of operations.

3. Once you have the formula worked out for the puzzle, get in there and see what happens when you modify the parts of the functions. Try to change it on purpose to make another value.

4. Do the inverse. Write a simple formula and use the functions in the same way to calculate it.

This exercise might really whack your brain out, but take it slow and easy and treat it like a little game. Figuring out puzzles like this is what makes programming fun, so I'll be giving you more little problems like this as we go.

Common Student Questions

Why does Python print the formula or the functions "backward"?   It's not really backward, it's "inside out." When you start breaking down the function into separate formulas and function calls you'll see how it works. Try to understand what I mean by "inside out" rather than "backward."

How can I use `input()` **to enter my own values?**   Remember `int(input())`? The problem with that is then you can't enter floating point, so also try using `float(input())` instead.

What do you mean by "write out a formula"?   Try `24 + 34 / 100 - 1023` as a start. Convert that to use the functions. Now come up with your own similar math equation, and use variables so it's more like a formula.

What Do You Know So Far?

There won't be any code in this exercise, so there's no *What You Should See* or *Study Drills* sections. In fact, this exercise is like one giant *Study Drills*. I'm going to have you do a review of what you have learned so far.

First, go back through every exercise you have done so far and write down every word and symbol (another name for "character") that you have used. Make sure your list of symbols is complete.

Next to each word or symbol, write its name and what it does. If you can't find a name for a symbol in this book, then look for it online. If you do not know what a word or symbol does, then read about it again and try using it in some code.

You may run into a few things you can't find out or know, so just keep those on the list and be ready to look them up when you find them.

Once you have your list, spend a few days rewriting the list and double-checking that it's correct. This may get boring, but push through and really nail it down.

Once you have memorized the list and what they do, then step it up by writing out tables of symbols, their names, and what they do *from memory*. If you hit some you can't recall from memory, go back and memorize them again.

> **WARNING!** The most important thing when doing this exercise is, "There is no failure, only trying."

What You Are Learning

It's important when you are doing a boring, mindless memorization exercise like this to know why. It helps you focus on a goal and know the purpose of all your efforts.

In this exercise you are learning the names of symbols so that you can read source code more easily. It's similar to learning the alphabet and basic words of English, except this Python alphabet has extra symbols you might not know.

Just take it slow and do not hurt your brain. It's best to take 15 minutes at a time with your list and then take a break. Giving your brain a rest will help you learn faster with less frustration.

Strings, Bytes, and Character Encodings

To do this exercise you'll need to *download* a text file that I've written named languages.txt (https://learnpythonthehardway.org/python3/languages.txt). This file was created with a list of human languages to demonstrate a few interesting concepts:

1. How modern computers store human languages for display and processing and how Python 3 calls this `strings`

2. How you must "encode" and "decode" Python's strings into a type called `bytes`

3. How to handle errors in your string and byte handling

4. How to read code and find out what it means even if you've never seen it before

In addition to that you'll also get a brief glimpse of the Python 3 `if-statement` and `lists` for processing a list of things. You don't have to master this code or understand these concepts right away. You'll get plenty of practice in later exercises. For now your job is to get a taste of the future and learn the four topics in the preceding list.

WARNING! This exercise is hard! There's a lot of information in it that you need to understand, and it's information that goes deep into computers. This exercise is complex because Python's strings are complex and difficult to use. I recommend you take this exercise *painfully* slow. Write down every word you don't understand, and look it up or research it. Take a paragraph at a time if you must. You can continue with other exercises while you study this one, so don't get stuck here. Just chip away at it for as long as it takes.

Initial Research

I'm going to teach you how to research a piece of code to expose its secrets. You'll need the languages.txt file for this code to work, so make sure you download it first. The `languages.txt` file simply contains a list of human language names that are encoded in UTF-8.

ex23.py

```
1   import sys
2   script, input_encoding, error = sys.argv
3
4
5   def main(language_file, encoding, errors):
6       line = language_file.readline()
7
```

```
8              if line:
9                  print_line(line, encoding, errors)
10                 return main(language_file, encoding, errors)
11
12
13     def print_line(line, encoding, errors):
14         next_lang = line.strip()
15         raw_bytes = next_lang.encode(encoding, errors=errors)
16         cooked_string = raw_bytes.decode(encoding, errors=errors)
17
18         print(raw_bytes, "<===>", cooked_string)
19
20
21     languages = open("languages.txt", encoding="utf-8")
22
23     main(languages, input_encoding, error)
```

Simply write down a list of each thing you've never seen before. There may be quite a few things that are new, so scan the file a few times.

Once you have that you'll want to run this Python script to play with it. Here are some example commands I used to test it:

```
python — bash — 80×24
$ python3.6 ex23.py utf-8 strict
b'Afrikaans' <===> Afrikaans
b'\xe1\x8a\xa0\xe1\x88\x9b\xe1\x88\xad\xe1\x8a\x9b' <===> አማርኛ
b'\xd0\x90\xd2\xa7\xd1\x81\xd1\x88\xd3\x99\xd0\xb0' <===> Аҧсшәа
b'\xd8\xa7\xd9\x84\xd8\xb9\xd8\xb1\xd8\xa8\xd9\x8a\xd8\xa9' <===> العربية
b'V\xc3\xb5ro' <===> Võro
b'\xe6\x96\x87\xe8\xa8\x80' <===> 文言
b'\xe5\x90\xb4\xe8\xaf\xad' <===> 吴语
b'\xd7\x99\xd7\x99\xd6\xb4\xd7\x93\xd7\x99\xd7\xaa' <===> ייִדיש
b'\xe4\xb8\xad\xe6\x96\x87' <===> 中文
$
```

WARNING! You'll notice I'm using images here to show you what you should see. After extensive testing it turns out that so many people have their computers configured to not display UTF-8 that I had to use images so you'll know what to expect. Even my own typesetting system (LaTeX) couldn't handle these encodings, forcing me to use images instead. If you don't see this then your Terminal is most likely not able to display UTF-8 and you should try to fix that.

These examples use the utf-8, utf-16, and big5 encodings to demonstrate the conversion and the types of errors you can get. Each of these names are called a "codec" in Python 3, but you use the parameter "encoding." At the end of this exercise there's a list of the available encodings if you want to try more. I'll cover what all of this output means shortly. You're only trying to get an idea of how this works so we can talk about it.

After you've run it a few times, go through your list of symbols and make a guess as to what they do. When you've written down your guesses try looking the symbols up online to see if you can confirm your hypotheses. Don't worry if you have no idea how to search for them. Just give it a try.

Switches, Conventions, and Encodings

Before I can get into what this code means, you need to learn some basics about how data is stored in a computer. Modern computers are incredibly complex, but at their cores they are like a huge array of light switches. Computers use electricity to flip switches on or off. These switches can represent 1 for on, or 0 for off. In the old days there were all kinds of weird computers that did more than just 1 or 0, but these days it's just 1s and 0s. One represents energy, electricity, on, power, substance. Zero represents off, done, gone, power down, the lack of energy. We call these 1s and 0s "bits."

Now, a computer that only lets you work with 1 and 0 would be both horribly inefficient and incredibly annoying. Computers take these 1s and 0s and use them to encode larger numbers. At the small end a computer will use 8 of these 1s and 0s to encode 256 numbers (0-255). What does "encode" mean, though? It's nothing more than an agreed-upon standard for how a sequence of bits should represent a number. It's a convention humans picked or stumbled on that says that 00000000 would be 0, 11111111 would be 255, and 00001111 would be 15. There were even huge wars in the early history of computers on nothing more than the order of these bits because they were simply conventions we all had to agree on.

Today we call a "byte" a sequence of 8 bits (1s and 0s). In the old days everyone had their own convention for a byte, so you'll still run into people who think that this term should be flexible and handle sequences of 9 bits, 7 bits, or 6 bits, but now we just say it's 8 bits. That's our convention, and that convention defines our encoding for a byte. There are futher conventions for encoding large numbers using 16, 32, 64, and even more bits if you get into really big math. There's entire standards groups who do nothing but argue about these conventions, then implement them as encodings that eventually turn switches on and off.

Once you have bytes you can start to store and display text by deciding on another convention for how a number maps to a letter. In the early days of computing there were many conventions that mapped 8 or 7 bits (or less or more) onto lists of characters kept inside a computer. The most popular convention ended up being American Standard Code for Information Interchange, or ASCII. This standard maps a number to a letter. The number 90 is Z, which in bits is 1011010, which gets mapped to the ASCII table inside the computer.

You can try this out in Python right now:

```
>>> 0b1011010
90
>>> ord('Z')
90
>>> chr(90)
'Z'
>>>
```

First, I write the number 90 in binary, then I get the number based on the letter 'Z', then I convert the number to the letter 'Z'. Don't worry about needing to remember this though. I think I've had to do it twice the entire time I've used Python.

Once we have the ASCII convention for encoding a character using 8 bits (a byte), we can then "string" them together to make a word. If I want to write my name, "Zed A. Shaw," I just use a sequence of bytes: [90, 101, 100, 32, 65, 46, 32, 83, 104, 97, 119]. Most of the early text in computers was nothing more than sequences of bytes, stored in memory, that a computer used to display text to a person. Again, this is just a sequence of conventions that turned switches on and off.

The problem with ASCII is that it only encodes English and maybe a few other similar languages. Remember that a byte can hold 256 numbers (0-255, or 00000000-11111111). Turns out, there's a *lot* more characters than 256 used throughout the world's languages. Different countries created their own encoding conventions for their languages, and that mostly worked, but many encodings could only handle one language. That meant if you want to put the title of an American English book in the middle of a Thai sentence you were kind of in trouble. You'd need one encoding for Thai and one for English.

To solve this problem a group of people created Unicode. It sounds like "encode," and it is meant to be a "universal encoding" of all human languages. The solution Unicode provides is like the ASCII table, but it's huge by comparison. You can use 32 bits to encode a Unicode character, and that is more characters than we could possibly find. A 32-bit number means we can store 4,294,967,295 characters (2^{32}), which is enough space for every possible human language and probably a lot of alien ones too. Right now we use the extra space for important things like poop and smile emojis.

We now have a convention for encoding any characters we want, but 32 bits is 4 bytes (32/8 == 4) which means there is so much wasted space in most text we want to encode. We can also use 16 bits (2 bytes), but still there's going to be wasted space in most text. The solution is to use a clever convention to encode most common characters using 8 bits, and then "escape" into larger numbers when we need to encode more characters. That means we have one more convention that is nothing more than a compression encoding, making it possible for most common characters to use 8 bits and then escape out into 16 or 32 bits as needed.

The convention for encoding text in Python is called "UTF-8", which means "Unicode Transformation Format 8 Bits." It is a convention for encoding Unicode characters into sequences of bytes, which are sequences of bits, which turn sequences of switches on and off. You can also use other conventions (encodings), but UTF-8 is the current standard.

Disecting the Output

We can now look at the output of the commands shown previously. Let's take just that first command and the first few lines of output:

```
● ● ●                        python — bash — 80×24
$ python3.6 ex23.py utf-8 strict
b'Afrikaans' <===> Afrikaans
b'\xe1\x8a\xa0\xe1\x88\x9b\xe1\x88\xad\xe1\x8a\x9b' <===> አማርኛ
b'\xd0\x90\xd2\xa7\xd1\x81\xd1\x88\xd3\x99\xd0\xb0' <===> Аҧсшәа
b'\xd8\xa7\xd9\x84\xd8\xb9\xd8\xb1\xd8\xa8\xd9\x8a\xd8\xa9' <===> العربية
b'V\xc3\xb5ro' <===> Võro
b'\xe6\x96\x87\xe8\xa8\x80' <===> 文言
b'\xe5\x90\xb4\xe8\xaf\xad' <===> 吴语
b'\xd7\x99\xd7\x99\xd6\xb4\xd7\x93\xd7\x99\xd7\xa9' <===> ייִדיש
b'\xe4\xb8\xad\xe6\x96\x87' <===> 中文
$ ▮
```

The ex23.py script is taking bytes written inside the b'' (byte string) and converting them to the UTF-8 (or other) encoding you specified. On the left is the numbers for each byte of the UTF-8 (shown in hexadecimal), and the right has the character output as actual UTF-8. The way to think of this is the left side of <===> is the Python numerical bytes, or the "raw" bytes Python uses to store the string. You specify this with b'' to tell Python this is bytes. These raw bytes are then displayed "cooked" on the right so you can see the real characters in your Terminal.

Disecting the Code

We have an understanding of strings and byte sequences. In Python a string is a UTF-8 encoded sequence of characters for displaying or working with text. The bytes are then the "raw" sequence of bytes that Python uses to store this UTF-8 string and start with a b' to tell Python you are working with raw bytes. This is all based on conventions for how Python wants to work with text. Here's a Python session showing me encoding strings and decoding bytes.

```
● ● ●                        python — bash — 82×34
$ python3.6
Python 3.6.0 (default, Feb  2 2017, 12:48:29)
[GCC 4.2.1 Compatible Apple LLVM 7.0.2 (clang-700.1.81)] on darwin
Type "help", "copyright", "credits" or "license" for more information.
>>> raw_bytes = b'\xe6\x96\x87\xe8\xa8\x80'
>>> utf_string = "文言"
>>> raw_bytes.decode()
'文言'
>>> utf_string.encode()
b'\xe6\x96\x87\xe8\xa8\x80'
>>> raw_bytes == utf_string.encode()
True
>>> utf_string == raw_bytes.decode()
True
>>>
>>> quit()
$ ▮
```

All you need to remember is if you have raw `bytes`, then you must use `.decode()` to get the `string`. Raw `bytes` have no convention to them. They are just sequences of bytes with no meaning other than numbers, so you must tell Python to "decode this into a UTF string." If you have a `string` and want to send it, store it, share it, or do some other operation, then usually it'll work, but sometimes Python will throw up an error saying it doesn't know how to "encode" it. Again, Python knows its internal convention, but it has no idea what convention you need. In that case, you must use `.encode()` to get the bytes you need.

The way to remember this (even though I look it up almost every time) is to remember the mnemonic DBES, which stands for *Decode Bytes, Encode Strings*. I say "deebess" in my head when I have to convert `bytes` and strings. When you have `bytes` and need a `string`, decode bytes. When you have a `string` and need `bytes`, encode strings.

With that in mind, let's break down the code in `ex23.py` line-by-line:

1–2   I start with the usual command line argument handling that you already know.

5   I start the main meat of this code in a function conveniently called `main`. This will be called at the end of this script to get things going.

6   The first thing this function does is read one line from the languages file it is given. You have done this before so nothing new here. Just `readline` as before when dealing with text files.

8   I use something new. You will learn about this in the second half of the book, so consider this a teaser of interesting things to come. This is an `if-statement`, and it lets you make decisions in your Python code. You can test the truth of a variable and, based on that truth, run a piece of code or not run it. In this case I'm testing whether `line` has something in it. The `readline` function will return an empty string when it reaches the end of the file and `if line` simply tests for this empty string. As long as `readline` gives us something, this will be true, and the code *under* (indented in, lines 9–10) will run. When this is false, Python will skip lines 9–10.

9   I call a separate function to do the actual printing of this line. This simplifies my code and makes it easier for me to understand it. If I want to learn what this function does, I can jump to it and study. Once I know what `print_line` does I can attach my memory to the name `print_line` and forget about the details.

10   I have written a tiny yet powerful piece of magic here. I am calling `main` again inside `main`. Actually it's not magic since nothing really is magical in programming. All the information you need is there. This looks like I am calling the function *inside* itself, which seems like it should be illegal to do. Ask yourself, why should that be illegal? There's no technical reason why I can't call any function I want right there, even this `main` function. If a function is simply a jump to the top where I've named it `main`, then calling this function at the end of itself would . . . jump back to the top and run it again. That would make it loop. Now look back at line 8, and you'll see the `if-statement` keeps this function from looping forever. Carefully study this because it is a significant concept, but don't worry if you can't grasp it right away.

13   I start the definition for the `print_line` function, which does the actual encoding of each line from the `languages.txt` file.

14   This is a simple stripping of the trailing `\n` on the `line` string.

15   I *finally* take the language I've received from the `languages.txt` file and encode it into the raw bytes. Remember the DBES mnemonic: Decode bytes, encode strings. The `next_lang` variable is a string, so to get the raw bytes I must call `.encode()` on it to encode strings. I pass to `encode()` the encoding I want and how to handle errors.

16   I do the extra step of showing the inverse of line 15 by creating a `cooked_string` variable from the `raw_bytes`. Remember, DBES says I decode bytes, and `raw_bytes` is bytes, so I call `.decode()` on it to get a Python `string`. This string should be the same as the `next_lang` variable.

18   I simply print them both out to show you what they look like.

21   I'm done defining functions, so now I want to open the `languages.txt` file.

23   The end of the script simply runs the `main` function with all the correct parameters to get everything going and kick-start the loop. Remember that this then jumps to where the `main` function is defined on line 5, and on line 10 `main` is called again, causing this to keep looping. The `if line:` on line 8 will prevent our loop from going forever.

Encodings Deep Dive

We can now use our little script to explore other encodings. The following shows me playing with different encodings and seeing how to break them. First, I'm doing a simple UTF-16 encoding so you can see how it changes compared to UTF-8. You can also use UTF-32 to see how that's even bigger and get an idea of the space saved with UTF-8. After that I try Big5, and you'll see that Python does *not* like that at all. It throws up an error that Big5 can't encode some of the characters at position 0 (which is super helpful). One solution is to tell Python to "replace" any bad characters for the Big5 encoding. That's the next example, and you'll see it puts a ? character wherever it finds a character that doesn't match the Big5 encoding system.

```
●  ●  ●                      📁 python — bash — 82×34
$ python3.6 ex23.py utf-16 strict
b'\xff\xfeA\x00f\x00r\x00i\x00k\x00a\x00a\x00n\x00s\x00' <===> Afrikaans
b'\xff\xfe\xa0\x12\x1b\x12-\x12\x9b\x12' <===> አማርኛ
b'\xff\xfe\x10\x04\xa7\x04A\x04H\x04\xd9\x040\x04' <===> Anɕwəa
b"\xff\xfe'\x06D\x069\x061\x06(\x06J\x06)\x06" <===> العربية
b'\xff\xfeV\x00\xf5\x00r\x00o\x00' <===> Võro
b'\xff\xfe\x87e\x00\x8a' <===> 文言
b'\xff\xfe4T\xed\x8b' <===> 吴语
b'\xff\xfe\xd9\x05\xd9\x05\xb4\x05\xd3\x05\xd9\x05\xe9\x05' <===> ייִדיש
b'\xff\xfe—N\x87e' <===> 中文
$ python3.6 ex23.py big5 strict
b'Afrikaans' <===> Afrikaans
Traceback (most recent call last):
  File "ex23.py", line 23, in <module>
    main(languages, encoding, error)
  File "ex23.py", line 10, in main
    return main(language_file, encoding, errors)
  File "ex23.py", line 9, in main
    print_line(line, encoding, errors)
  File "ex23.py", line 15, in print_line
    raw_bytes = next_lang.encode(encoding, errors=errors)
UnicodeEncodeError: 'big5' codec can't encode character '\u12a0' in position 0: il
legal multibyte sequence
$ python3.6 ex23.py big5 replace
b'Afrikaans' <===> Afrikaans
b'????' <===> ????
b'??\xc7\xda\xc7\xe1?\xc7\xc8' <===> ??cɰ?a
b'???????' <===> ???????
b'V?ro' <===> V?ro
b'\xa4\xe5\xa8\xa5' <===> 文言
b'??' <===> ??
b'??????' <===> ??????
b'\xa4\xa4\xa4\xe5' <===> 中文
$ ▊
```

Breaking It

Rough ideas include the following:

1. Find strings of text encoded in other encodings and place them in the ex23.py file to see how it breaks.

2. Find out what happens when you give an encoding that doesn't exist.

3. Extra challenging: Rewrite this using the b'' bytes instead of the UTF-8 strings, effectively reversing the script.

4. If you can do that, then you can also *break* these bytes by removing some to see what happens. How much do you need to remove to cause Python to break? How much can you remove to damage the string output but pass Python's decoding system.

5. Use what you learned from item 4 to see if you can mangle the files. What errors do you get? How much damage can you cause and get the file past Python's decoding system?

More Practice

You are getting to the end of this section. You should have enough Python "under your fingers" to move on to learning about how programming really works, but you should do some more practice. This exercise is longer and all about building up stamina. The next exercise will be similar. Do them, get them exactly right, and do your checks.

ex24.py

```
1    print("Let's practice everything.")
2    print('You\'d need to know \'bout escapes with \\ that do:')
3    print('\n newlines and \t tabs.')
4
5    poem = """
6    \tThe lovely world
7    with logic so firmly planted
8    cannot discern \n the needs of love
9    nor comprehend passion from intuition
10   and requires an explanation
11   \n\t\twhere there is none.
12   """
13
14   print("--------------")
15   print(poem)
16   print("--------------")
17
18
19   five = 10 - 2 + 3 - 6
20   print(f"This should be five: {five}")
21
22   def secret_formula(started):
23       jelly_beans = started * 500
24       jars = jelly_beans / 1000
25       crates = jars / 100
26       return jelly_beans, jars, crates
27
28
29   start_point = 10000
30   beans, jars, crates = secret_formula(start_point)
31
32   # remember that this is another way to format a string
33   print("With a starting point of: {}".format(start_point))
34   # it's just like with an f"" string
35   print(f"We'd have {beans} beans, {jars} jars, and {crates} crates.")
36
37   start_point = start_point / 10
```

```
38
39    print("We can also do that this way:")
40    formula = secret_formula(start_point)
41    # this is an easy way to apply a list to a format string
42    print("We'd have {} beans, {} jars, and {} crates.".format(*formula))
```

What You Should See

```
$ python3.6 ex24.py
Let's practice everything.
You'd need to know 'bout escapes with \ that do:

 newlines and        tabs.
--------------

   The lovely world
with logic so firmly planted
cannot discern
 the needs of love
nor comprehend passion from intuition
and requires an explanation

          where there is none.

--------------
This should be five: 5
With a starting point of: 10000
We'd have 5000000 beans, 5000.0 jars, and 50.0 crates.
We can also do that this way:
We'd have 500000.0 beans, 500.0 jars, and 5.0 crates.
```

Study Drills

1. Make sure to do your checks: read it backward, read it out loud, and put comments above confusing parts.

2. Break the file on purpose, then run it to see what kinds of errors you get. Make sure you can fix it.

Common Student Questions

Why do you call the variable jelly_beans **but the name** beans **later?** That's part of how a function works. Remember that inside the function the variable is temporary. When you return it then it can be assigned to a variable for later. I'm just making a new variable named beans to hold the return value.

What do you mean by reading the code backward? Start at the last line. Compare that line in your file to the same line in mine. Once it's exactly the same, move up to the next line. Do this until you get to the first line of the file.

Who wrote that poem? I did. Not all of my poems suck.

Even More Practice

We're going to do some more practice involving functions and variables to make sure you know them well. This exercise should be straightforward for you to type in, break down, and understand.

However, this exercise is a little different. You won't be running it. Instead *you* will import it into Python and run the functions yourself.

ex25.py

```python
def break_words(stuff):
    """This function will break up words for us."""
    words = stuff.split(' ')
    return words

def sort_words(words):
    """Sorts the words."""
    return sorted(words)

def print_first_word(words):
    """Prints the first word after popping it off."""
    word = words.pop(0)
    print(word)

def print_last_word(words):
    """Prints the last word after popping it off."""
    word = words.pop(-1)
    print(word)

def sort_sentence(sentence):
    """Takes in a full sentence and returns the sorted words."""
    words = break_words(sentence)
    return sort_words(words)

def print_first_and_last(sentence):
    """Prints the first and last words of the sentence."""
    words = break_words(sentence)
    print_first_word(words)
    print_last_word(words)

def print_first_and_last_sorted(sentence):
    """Sorts the words then prints the first and last one."""
    words = sort_sentence(sentence)
    print_first_word(words)
    print_last_word(words)
```

First, run this with `python3.6 ex25.py` to find any errors you have made. Once you have found all of the errors you can and fixed them, you will then want to follow the *What You Should See* section to complete the exercise.

What You Should See

In this exercise we're going to interact with your `ex25.py` file inside the `python3.6` interpreter you used periodically to do calculations. You run `python3.6` from the Terminal like this:

```
$ python3.6
Python 3.6.0rc2 (v3.6.0rc2:800a67f7806d, Dec 16 2016, 14:12:21)
[GCC 4.2.1 (Apple Inc. build 5666) (dot 3)] on darwin
Type "help", "copyright", "credits" or "license" for more information.
>>>
```

Your output should look like mine, and after the > character (called the prompt) you can type Python code in, and it will run immediately. Using this I want you to type each of these lines of Python code into `python3.6` and see what it does:

Exercise 25 Python Session

```
 1    import ex25
 2    sentence = "All good things come to those who wait."
 3    words = ex25.break_words(sentence)
 4    words
 5    sorted_words = ex25.sort_words(words)
 6    sorted_words
 7    ex25.print_first_word(words)
 8    ex25.print_last_word(words)
 9    words
10    ex25.print_first_word(sorted_words)
11    ex25.print_last_word(sorted_words)
12    sorted_words
13    sorted_words = ex25.sort_sentence(sentence)
14    sorted_words
15    ex25.print_first_and_last(sentence)
16    ex25.print_first_and_last_sorted(sentence)
```

Here's what it looks like when I work with the `ex25.py` module in `python3.6`:

Exercise 25 Python Session

```
Python 3.6.0 (default, Feb  2 2017, 12:48:29)
[GCC 4.2.1 Compatible Apple LLVM 7.0.2 (clang-700.1.81)] on darwin
Type "help", "copyright", "credits" or "license" for more information.
>>> import ex25
>>> sentence = "All good things come to those who wait."
>>> words = ex25.break_words(sentence)
```

```
>>> words
['All', 'good', 'things', 'come', 'to', 'those', 'who', 'wait.']
>>> sorted_words = ex25.sort_words(words)
>>> sorted_words
['All', 'come', 'good', 'things', 'those', 'to', 'wait.', 'who']
>>> ex25.print_first_word(words)
All
>>> ex25.print_last_word(words)
wait.
>>> words
['good', 'things', 'come', 'to', 'those', 'who']
>>> ex25.print_first_word(sorted_words)
All
>>> ex25.print_last_word(sorted_words)
who
>>> sorted_words
['come', 'good', 'things', 'those', 'to', 'wait.']
>>> sorted_words = ex25.sort_sentence(sentence)
>>> sorted_words
['All', 'come', 'good', 'things', 'those', 'to', 'wait.', 'who']
>>> ex25.print_first_and_last(sentence)
All
wait.
>>> ex25.print_first_and_last_sorted(sentence)
All
who
```

As you go through each of these lines, make sure you can find the function that's being run in ex25.py and understand how each one works. If you get different results or error, you'll have to go fix your code, exit python3.6, and start over.

Study Drills

1. Take the remaining lines of the *What You Should See* output and figure out what they are doing. Make sure you understand how you are running your functions in the ex25 module.

2. Try doing this: help(ex25) and also help(ex25.break_words). Notice how you get help for your module and how the help is those odd " " " strings you put after each function in ex25? Those special strings are called *documentation comments*, and we'll be seeing more of them.

3. Typing ex25. is annoying. A shortcut is to do your import like this: from ex25 import *. This is like saying, "Import everything from ex25." Programmers like saying things backward. Start a new session and see how all your functions are right there.

4. Try breaking your file and see what it looks like in python when you use it. You will have to quit python with quit() to be able to reload it.

Common Student Questions

I get None **printed out for some of the functions.** You probably have a function that is missing the return at the end. Go backward through the file and confirm that every line is right.

I get -bash: import: command not found **when I type** import ex25. Pay attention to what I'm doing in the *What You Should See* section. I'm doing this in *Python*, not in the Terminal. That means you first run Python.

I get ImportError: No module named ex25.py **when I type** import ex25.py. Don't add the .py to the end. Python knows the file ends in .py, so you just type import ex25.

I get SyntaxError: invalid syntax **when I run this.** That means you have something like a missing (or " or similar syntax error on that line or above it. Any time you get that error, start at the line it mentions and check that it's right, then go backward checking each line above that.

How can the words.pop **function change the** words **variable?** That's a complicated question, but in this case words is a list, and because of that you can give it commands, and it'll retain the results of those commands. This is similar to how files and many other things worked when you were working with them.

When should I print **instead of** return **in a function?** The return from a function gives the line of code that called the function a result. You can think of a function as taking input through its arguments and returning output through return. The print is *completely* unrelated to this and only deals with printing output to the Terminal.

Congratulations, Take a Test!

You are almost done with the first half of the book. The second half is where things get interesting. You will learn logic and be able to do useful things like make decisions.

Before you continue, I have a quiz for you. This quiz will be *very* hard because it requires you to fix someone else's code. When you are a programmer you often have to deal with other programmers' code—and also with their arrogance. Programmers will very frequently claim that their code is perfect.

These programmers are stupid people who care little for others. A good programmer assumes, like a good scientist, that there's always *some* probability their code is wrong. Good programmers start from the premise that their software is broken and then work to rule out all possible ways it could be wrong before finally admitting that maybe it really is the other guy's code.

In this exercise, you will practice dealing with a bad programmer by fixing a bad programmer's code. I have poorly copied Exercises 24 and 25 into a file and removed random characters and added flaws. Most of the errors are things Python will tell you, while some of them are math errors you should find. Others are formatting errors or spelling mistakes in the strings.

All of these errors are very common mistakes all programmers make—even experienced ones.

Your job in this exercise is to correct this file. Use all of your skills to make this file better. Analyze it first, maybe printing it out to edit it like you would a school term paper. Fix each flaw and keep running it and fixing it until the script runs perfectly. Try not to get help. If you get stuck, take a break and come back to it later.

Even if this takes days to do, bust through it and make it right.

The point of this exercise isn't to type it in but to fix an existing file. To do that, you must go to http://learnpythonthehardway.org/python3/exercise26.txt. Copy-paste the code into a file named `ex26.py`. This is the only time you are allowed to copy-paste.

Common Student Questions

Do I have to import `ex25.py`, **or can I just remove the references to it?** You can do either. This file has the functions from ex25 though, so first go with removing references to it.

Can I run the code while I'm fixing it? You most certainly may. The computer is there to help, so use it as much as possible.

Memorizing Logic

T oday is the day you start learning about logic. Up to this point you have done everything you possibly can reading and writing files to the Terminal, and have learned quite a lot of the math capabilities of Python.

From now on, you will be learning *logic*. You won't learn complex theories that academics love to study but just the basic logic that makes real programs work and that real programmers need every day.

Learning logic has to come after you do some memorization. I want you to do this exercise for an entire week. Do not falter. Even if you are bored out of your mind, keep doing it. This exercise has a set of logic tables you must memorize to make it easier for you to do the later exercises.

I'm warning you this won't be fun at first. It will be downright boring and tedious, but this teaches you a very important skill you will need as a programmer. You *will* need to be able to memorize important concepts in your life. Most of these concepts will be exciting once you get them. You will struggle with them, like wrestling a squid, then one day you will understand it. All that work memorizing the basics pays off big later.

Here's a tip on how to memorize something without going insane: Do a tiny bit at a time throughout the day and mark down what you need to work on most. Do not try to sit down for two hours straight and memorize these tables. This won't work. Your brain will only retain whatever you studied in the first 15 or 30 minutes anyway. Instead, create a bunch of index cards with each column on the left (True or False) on the front, and the column on the right on the back. You should then take them out, see the "True or False" and immediately say "True!" Keep practicing until you can do this.

Once you can do that, start writing out your own truth tables each night into a notebook. Do not just copy them. Try to do them from memory. When you get stuck, glance quickly at the ones I have here to refresh your memory. Doing this will train your brain to remember the whole table.

Do not spend more than one week on this, because you will be applying it as you go.

The Truth Terms

In Python we have the following terms (characters and phrases) for determining if something is "True" or "False." Logic on a computer is all about seeing if some combination of these characters and some variables is True at that point in the program.

- `and`
- `or`
- `not`

- != (not equal)
- == (equal)
- >= (greater-than-equal)
- <= (less-than-equal)
- `True`
- `False`

You actually have run into these characters before but maybe not the terms. The terms (`and`, `or`, `not`) actually work the way you expect them to, just like in English.

The Truth Tables

We will now use these characters to make the truth tables you need to memorize.

NOT	True?
not False	True
not True	False

OR	True?
True or False	True
True or True	True
False or True	True
False or False	False

AND	True?
True and False	False
True and True	True
False and True	False
False and False	False

NOT OR	True?
not (True or False)	False
not (True or True)	False
not (False or True)	False
not (False or False)	True

NOT AND	True?
not (True and False)	True
not (True and True)	False
not (False and True)	True
not (False and False)	True

!=	True?
1 != 0	True
1 != 1	False
0 != 1	True
0 != 0	False

==	True?
1 == 0	False
1 == 1	True
0 == 1	False
0 == 0	True

Now use these tables to write up your own cards and spend the week memorizing them. Remember, though, there is no failing in this book, just trying as hard as you can each day, and then a *little* bit more.

Common Student Questions

Can't I just learn the concepts behind Boolean algebra and not memorize this?   Sure, you can do that, but then you'll have to constantly go through the rules for Boolean algebra while you code. If you memorize these first, it not only builds your memorization skills, it also makes these operations natural. After that, the concept of Boolean algebra is easy. But do whatever works for you.

Boolean Practice

The logic combinations you learned from the last exercise are called *Boolean logic* expressions. Boolean logic is used *everywhere* in programming. It is a fundamental part of computation, and knowing the expressions is akin to knowing your scales in music.

In this exercise you will take the logic exercises you memorized and start trying them out in Python. Take each of these logic problems and write what you think the answer will be. In each case it will be either True or False. Once you have the answers written down, start Python in your Terminal and type each logic problem in to confirm your answers.

1. True and True
2. False and True
3. 1 == 1 and 2 == 1
4. "test" == "test"
5. 1 == 1 or 2 != 1
6. True and 1 == 1
7. False and 0 != 0
8. True or 1 == 1
9. "test" == "testing"
10. 1 != 0 and 2 == 1
11. "test" != "testing"
12. "test" == 1
13. not (True and False)
14. not (1 == 1 and 0 != 1)
15. not (10 == 1 or 1000 == 1000)
16. not (1 != 10 or 3 == 4)
17. not ("testing" == "testing" and "Zed" == "Cool Guy")
18. 1 == 1 and (not ("testing" == 1 or 1 == 0))
19. "chunky" == "bacon" and (not (3 == 4 or 3 == 3))
20. 3 == 3 and (not ("testing" == "testing" or "Python" == "Fun"))

I will also give you a trick to help you figure out the more complicated ones toward the end.

Whenever you see these Boolean logic statements, you can solve them easily by this simple process:

1. Find an equality test (== or !=) and replace it with its truth.
2. Find each and/or inside parentheses and solve those first.
3. Find each not and invert it.
4. Find any remaining and/or and solve it.
5. When you are done you should have True or False.

I will demonstrate with a variation on item 20:

```
3 != 4 and not ("testing" != "test" or "Python" == "Python")
```

Here's me going through each of the steps and showing you the translation until I've boiled it down to a single result:

1. Solve each equality test:

   `3 != 4` is True: `True and not ("testing" != "test" or "Python" == "Python")`

   `"testing" != "test"` is True: `True and not (True or "Python" == "Python")`

   `"Python" == "Python"`: `True and not (True or True)`

2. Find each and/or in parentheses ():

   `(True or True)` is True: `True and not (True)`

3. Find each not and invert it:

   `not (True)` is False: `True and False`

4. Find any remaining and/ors and solve them:

   `True and False` is False

With that we're done and know the result is False.

WARNING! The more complicated ones may seem *very* hard at first. You should be able to take a good first stab at solving them, but do not get discouraged. I'm just getting you primed for more of these "logic gymnastics" so that later cool stuff is much easier. Just stick with it, and keep track of what you get wrong, but do not worry that it's not getting in your head quite yet. It'll come.

What You Should See

After you have tried to guess at these, this is what your session with Python might look like:

```
$ python3.6
Python 2.5.1 (r251:54863, Feb  6 2009, 19:02:12)
[GCC 4.0.1 (Apple Inc. build 5465)] on darwin
Type "help", "copyright", "credits" or "license" for more information.
>>> True and True
True
>>> 1 == 1 and 2 == 2
True
```

Study Drills

1. There are a lot of operators in Python similar to != and ==. Try to find as many "equality operators" as you can. They should be like < or <=.

2. Write out the names of each of these equality operators. For example, I call != "not equal."

3. Play with Python by typing out new Boolean operators, and before you press Enter try to shout out what it is. Do not think about it. Shout the first thing that comes to mind. Write it down, then press Enter, and keep track of how many you get right and wrong.

4. Throw away the piece of paper from 3 so you do not accidentally try to use it later.

Common Student Questions

Why does "test" and "test" **return** "test" **or** 1 and 1 **return** 1 **instead of** True?   Python and many languages like to return one of the operands to their Boolean expressions rather than just True or False. This means that if you did False and 1 you get the first operand (False), but if you do True and 1 you get the second (1). Play with this a bit.

Is there any difference between != **and** <>?   Python has deprecated <> in favor of !=, so use !=. Other than that there should be no difference.

Isn't there a shortcut?   Yes. Any and expression that has a False is immediately False, so you can stop there. Any or expression that has a True is immediately True, so you can stop there. But make sure that you can process the whole expression because later it becomes helpful.

What If

Here is the next script of Python you will enter, which introduces you to the `if-statement`. Type this in, make it run exactly right, and then we'll see if your practice has paid off.

ex29.py

```
 1    people = 20
 2    cats = 30
 3    dogs = 15
 4
 5
 6    if people < cats:
 7        print("Too many cats! The world is doomed!")
 8
 9    if people > cats:
10        print("Not many cats! The world is saved!")
11
12    if people < dogs:
13        print("The world is drooled on!").
14
15    if people > dogs:
16        print("The world is dry!")
17
18
19    dogs += 5
20
21    if people >= dogs:
22        print("People are greater than or equal to dogs.")
23
24    if people <= dogs:
25        print("People are less than or equal to dogs.")
26
27
28    if people == dogs:
29        print("People are dogs.")
```

What You Should See

Exercise 29 Session

```
$ python3.6 ex29.py
Too many cats! The world is doomed!
The world is dry!
People are greater than or equal to dogs.
People are less than or equal to dogs.
People are dogs.
```

Study Drills

In this Study Drill, try to guess what you think the if-statement is and what it does. Try to answer these questions in your own words before moving on to the next exercise:

1. What do you think the if does to the code under it?
2. Why does the code under the if need to be indented four spaces?
3. What happens if it isn't indented?
4. Can you put other Boolean expressions from Exercise 27 in the if-statement? Try it.
5. What happens if you change the initial values for people, cats, and dogs?

Common Student Questions

What does += mean?   The code x += 1 is the same as doing x = x + 1 but involves less typing. You can call this the "increment by" operator. The same goes for -= and many other expressions you'll learn later.

Else and If

In the last exercise you worked out some if-statements and then tried to guess what they are and how they work. Before you learn more I'll explain what everything is by answering the questions you had from the previous *Study Drills* section. You did the *Study Drills*, right?

1. What do you think the if does to the code under it? An if-statement creates what is called a "branch" in the code. It's kind of like those choose your own adventure books where you are asked to turn to one page if you make one choice and another if you go a different direction. The if-statement tells your script, "If this Boolean expression is True, then run the code under it; otherwise, skip it."

2. Why does the code under the if need to be indented four spaces? A colon at the end of a line is how you tell Python you are going to create a new "block" of code, and then indenting four spaces tells Python what lines of code are in that block. This is *exactly* the same thing you did when you made functions in the first half of the book.

3. What happens if it isn't indented? If it isn't indented, you will most likely create a Python error. Python expects you to indent *something* after you end a line with a : (colon).

4. Can you put other Boolean expressions from Exercise 27 in the if-statement? Try it. Yes, you can, and they can be as complex as you like, although really complex things generally are bad style.

5. What happens if you change the initial values for people, cats, and dogs? Because you are comparing numbers, if you change the numbers, different if-statements will evaluate to True and the blocks of code under them will run. Go back and put different numbers in and see if you can figure out in your head which blocks of code will run.

Compare my answers to your answers, and make sure you *really* understand the concept of a "block" of code. This is important for when you do the next exercise where you write all the parts of if-statements that you can use.

Type this one in and make it work too.

ex30.py

```
1    people = 30
2    cars = 40
3    trucks = 15
4
5
6    if cars > people:
7        print("We should take the cars.")
```

```
 8    elif cars < people:
 9        print("We should not take the cars.")
10    else:
11        print("We can't decide.")
12
13    if trucks > cars:
14        print("That's too many trucks.")
15    elif trucks < cars:
16        print("Maybe we could take the trucks.")
17    else:
18        print("We still can't decide.")
19
20    if people > trucks:
21        print("Alright, let's just take the trucks.")
22    else:
23        print("Fine, let's stay home then.")
```

What You Should See

```
$ python3.6 ex30.py
We should take the cars.
Maybe we could take the trucks.
Alright, let's just take the trucks.
```

Study Drills

1. Try to guess what elif and else are doing.

2. Change the numbers of cars, people, and trucks, and then trace through each if-statement to see what will be printed.

3. Try some more complex Boolean expressions like cars > people or trucks < cars.

4. Above each line write a comment describing what the line does.

Common Student Questions

What happens if multiple elif blocks are True?   Python starts at the top and runs the first block that is True, so it will run only the first one.

Making Decisions

In the first half of this book you mostly just printed out strings and called functions, but everything was basically in a straight line. Your scripts ran starting at the top and went to the bottom where they ended. If you made a function, you could run that function later, but it still didn't have the kind of branching you need to really make decisions. Now that you have if, else, and elif you can start to make scripts that decide things.

In the last script you wrote out a simple set of tests asking some questions. In this script you will ask the user questions and make decisions based on their answers. Write this script, and then play with it quite a lot to figure it out.

ex31.py

```
1   print("""You enter a dark room with two doors.
2   Do you go through door #1 or door #2?""")
3
4   door = input("> ")
5
6   if door == "1":
7       print("There's a giant bear here eating a cheese cake.")
8       print("What do you do?")
9       print("1. Take the cake.")
10      print("2. Scream at the bear.")
11
12      bear = input("> ")
13
14      if bear == "1":
15          print("The bear eats your face off.  Good job!")
16      elif bear == "2":
17          print("The bear eats your legs off.  Good job!")
18      else:
19          print(f"Well, doing {bear} is probably better.")
20          print("Bear runs away.")
21
22  elif door == "2":
23      print("You stare into the endless abyss at Cthulhu's retina.")
24      print("1. Blueberries.")
25      print("2. Yellow jacket clothespins.")
26      print("3. Understanding revolvers yelling melodies.")
27
28      insanity = input("> ")
29
30      if insanity == "1" or insanity == "2":
31          print("Your body survives powered by a mind of jello.")
```

```
32              print("Good job!")
33          else:
34              print("The insanity rots your eyes into a pool of muck.")
35              print("Good job!")
36
37      else:
38          print("You stumble around and fall on a knife and die.  Good job!")
```

A key point here is that you are now putting the `if-statements` *inside* `if-statements` as code that can run. This is very powerful and can be used to create "nested" decisions, where one branch leads to another and another.

Make sure you understand this concept of `if-statements` inside `if-statements`. In fact, do the *Study Drills* to really nail it.

What You Should See

Here is me playing this little adventure game. I do not do so well.

```
$ python3.6 ex31.py
You enter a dark room with two doors.
Do you go through door #1 or door #2?
>  1
There's a giant bear here eating a cheese cake.
What do you do?
1. Take the cake.
2. Scream at the bear.
>  2
The bear eats your legs off.  Good job!
```

Study Drills

1. Make new parts of the game and change what decisions people can make. Expand the game out as much as you can before it gets ridiculous.

2. Write a completely new game. Maybe you don't like this one, so make your own. This is your computer; do what you want.

Common Student Questions

Can you replace `elif` with a sequence of `if-else` combinations?   You can in some situations, but it depends on how each if/else is written. It also means that Python will check *every* `if-else` combination, rather than just the first false ones like it would with `if-elif-else`. Try to make some of these to figure out the differences.

How do I tell whether a number is between a range of numbers?   You have two options: Use `0 < x < 10` or `1 <= x < 10`, which is classic notation, or use `x in range(1, 10)`.

What if I wanted more options in the `if-elif-else` blocks?   Add more `elif` blocks for each possible choice.

Loops and Lists

You should now be able to do some programs that are much more interesting. If you have been keeping up, you should realize that now you can combine all the other things you have learned with if-statements and Boolean expressions to make your programs do smart things.

However, programs also need to do repetitive things very quickly. We are going to use a for-loop in this exercise to build and print various lists. When you do the exercise, you will start to figure out what they are. I won't tell you right now. You have to figure it out.

Before you can use a for-loop, you need a way to *store* the results of loops somewhere. The best way to do this is with lists. A list is exactly what the name says: a container of things that are organized in order from first to last. It's not complicated; you just have to learn a new syntax. First, here's how you make lists:

```
hairs = ['brown', 'blond', 'red']
eyes = ['brown', 'blue', 'green']
weights = [1, 2, 3, 4]
```

You start the list with the [(left bracket) which "opens" the list. Then you put each item you want in the list separated by commas, similar to function arguments. Lastly, end the list with a] (right bracket) to indicate that it's over. Python then takes this list and all its contents and assigns them to the variable.

WARNING! This is where things get tricky for people who can't code. Your brain has been taught that the world is flat. Remember in the last exercise where you put if-statements inside if-statements? That probably made your brain hurt because most people do not ponder how to "nest" things inside things. In programming nested structures are all over the place. You will find functions that call other functions that have if-statements that have lists with lists inside lists. If you see a structure like this that you can't figure out, take out a pencil and paper and break it down manually bit by bit until you understand it.

We now will build some lists using some for-loops and print them out:

ex32.py

```
1    the_count = [1, 2, 3, 4, 5]
2    fruits = ['apples', 'oranges', 'pears', 'apricots']
3    change = [1, 'pennies', 2, 'dimes', 3, 'quarters']
4
5    # this first kind of for-loop goes through a list
```

```
6    for number in the_count:
7        print(f"This is count {number}")
8
9    # same as above
10   for fruit in fruits:
11       print(f"A fruit of type: {fruit}")
12
13   # also we can go through mixed lists too
14   # notice we have to use {} since we don't know what's in it
15   for i in change:
16       print(f"I got {i}")
17
18   # we can also build lists, first start with an empty one
19   elements = []
20
21   # then use the range function to do 0 to 5 counts
22   for i in range(0, 6):
23       print(f"Adding {i} to the list.")
24       # append is a function that lists understand
25       elements.append(i)
26
27   # now we can print them out too
28   for i in elements:
29       print(f"Element was: {i}")
```

What You Should See

```
$ python3.6 ex32.py
This is count 1
This is count 2
This is count 3
This is count 4
This is count 5
A fruit of type: apples
A fruit of type: oranges
A fruit of type: pears
A fruit of type: apricots
I got 1
I got pennies
I got 2
I got dimes
I got 3
I got quarters
Adding 0 to the list.
Adding 1 to the list.
Adding 2 to the list.
Adding 3 to the list.
```

```
Adding 4 to the list.
Adding 5 to the list.
Element was: 0
Element was: 1
Element was: 2
Element was: 3
Element was: 4
Element was: 5
```

Study Drills

1. Take a look at how you used `range`. Look up the `range` function to understand it.

2. Could you have avoided that `for-loop` entirely on line 22 and just assigned `range(0,6)` directly to `elements`?

3. Find the Python documentation on lists and read about them. What other operations can you do to lists besides `append`?

Common Student Questions

How do you make a 2-dimensional (2D) list?   That's a list in a list, like this: `[[1,2,3],[4,5,6]]`.

Aren't lists and arrays the same thing?   That depends on the language and the implementation. In classic terms a list is very different from an array because of how they're implemented. In Ruby, though, they call these arrays. In Python they call them lists. Just call these lists for now since that's what Python calls them.

Why is a `for-loop` able to use a variable that isn't defined yet?   The variable is defined by the `for-loop` when it starts, initializing it to the current element of the loop iteration each time through.

Why does `for i in range(1, 3):` only loop two times instead of three times?   The `range()` function only does numbers from the first to the last, *not including the last*. So it stops at two, not three, in the preceding. This turns out to be the most common way to do this kind of loop.

What does `elements.append()` do?   It simply appends to the end of the list. Open up the Python shell and try a few examples with a list you make. Any time you run into things like this, always try to play with them interactively in the Python shell.

While Loops

N ow to totally blow your mind with a new loop, the while-loop. A while-loop will keep executing the code block under it as long as a Boolean expression is True.

Wait, you have been keeping up with the terminology, right? That if we write a line and end it with a : (colon) then that tells Python to start a new block of code? Then we indent and that's the new code. This is all about structuring your programs so that Python knows what you mean. If you do not get that idea then go back and do some more work with if-statements, functions, and the for-loop until you get it.

Later on we'll have some exercises that will train your brain to read these structures, similar to how we burned Boolean expressions into your brain.

Back to while-loops. What they do is simply do a test like an if-statement, but instead of running the code block *once*, they jump back to the "top" where the while is and repeat. A while-loop runs until the expression is False.

Here's the problem with while-loops: Sometimes they do not stop. This is great if your intention is to just keep looping until the end of the universe. Otherwise, you almost always want your loops to end eventually.

To avoid these problems, there are some rules to follow:

1. Make sure that you use while-loops sparingly. Usually a for-loop is better.

2. Review your while statements and make sure that the Boolean test will become False at some point.

3. When in doubt, print out your test variable at the top and bottom of the while-loop to see what it's doing.

In this exercise, you learn the while-loop while doing these three checks:

ex33.py

```
1   i = 0
2   numbers = []
3
4   while i < 6:
5       print(f"At the top i is {i}")
6       numbers.append(i)
7
8       i = i + 1
9       print("Numbers now: ", numbers)
```

```
10          print(f"At the bottom i is {i}")
11
12
13      print("The numbers: ")
14
15      for num in numbers:
16          print(num)
```

What You Should See

Exercise 33 Session

```
$ python3.6 ex33.py
At the top i is 0
Numbers now:  [0]
At the bottom i is 1
At the top i is 1
Numbers now:  [0, 1]
At the bottom i is 2
At the top i is 2
Numbers now:  [0, 1, 2]
At the bottom i is 3
At the top i is 3
Numbers now:  [0, 1, 2, 3]
At the bottom i is 4
At the top i is 4
Numbers now:  [0, 1, 2, 3, 4]
At the bottom i is 5
At the top i is 5
Numbers now:  [0, 1, 2, 3, 4, 5]
At the bottom i is 6
The numbers:
0
1
2
3
4
5
```

Study Drills

1. Convert this while-loop to a function that you can call, and replace 6 in the test (i < 6) with a variable.

2. Use this function to rewrite the script to try different numbers.

3. Add another variable to the function arguments that you can pass in that lets you change the + 1 on line 8 so you can change how much it increments by.

4. Rewrite the script again to use this function to see what effect that has.

5. Write it to use `for-loops` and `range`. Do you need the incrementor in the middle anymore? What happens if you do not get rid of it?

If at any time you are doing this it goes crazy (it probably will), just hold down CTRL and press c (CTRL-c) and the program will abort.

Common Student Questions

What's the difference between a `for-loop` **and a** `while-loop`? A `for-loop` can only iterate (loop) "over" collections of things. A `while-loop` can do any kind of iteration (looping) you want. However, `while-loops` are harder to get right, and you normally can get many things done with `for-loops`.

Loops are hard. How do I figure them out? The main reason people don't understand loops is because they can't follow the "jumping" that the code does. When a loop runs, it goes through its block of code, and at the end it jumps back to the top. To visualize this, put `print` statements all over the loop printing out where in the loop Python is running and what the variables are set to at those points. Write `print` lines before the loop, at the top of the loop, in the middle, and at the bottom. Study the output and try to understand the jumping that's going on.

Accessing Elements of Lists

Lists are pretty useful, but unless you can get at the things in them, they aren't all that good. You can already go through the elements of a list in order, but what if you want say, the fifth element? You need to know how to access the elements of a list. Here's how you would access the *first* element of a list:

```
animals = ['bear', 'tiger', 'penguin', 'zebra']
bear = animals[0]
```

You take a list of animals, and then you get the first (1st) one using 0?! How does that work? Because of the way math works, Python starts its lists at 0 rather than 1. It seems weird, but there are many advantages to this, even though it is mostly arbitrary.

The best way to explain why is by showing you the difference between how you use numbers and how programmers use numbers.

Imagine you are watching the four animals in our list (['bear', 'tiger', 'penguin', 'zebra']) run in a race. They cross the finish line in the *order* we have them in this list. The race was really exciting because the animals didn't eat each other and somehow managed to run a race. Your friend shows up late and wants to know who won. Does your friend say, "Hey, who came in *zeroth*?" No, he says, "Hey, who came in *first*?"

This is because the *order* of the animals is important. You can't have the second animal without the first (1st) animal, and you can't have the third without the second. It's also impossible to have a "zeroth" animal, since zero means nothing. How can you have a nothing win a race? It just doesn't make sense. We call these kinds of numbers "ordinal" numbers, because they indicate an ordering of things.

Programmers, however, can't think this way, because they can pick any element out of a list at any point. To programmers, the list of animals is more like a deck of cards. If they want the tiger, they grab it. If they want the zebra, they can take it, too. This need to pull elements out of lists at random means that they need a way to indicate elements consistently by an address, or an "index," and the best way to do that is to start the indices at 0. Trust me on this: the math is *way* easier for these kinds of accesses. This kind of number is a "cardinal" number and means you can pick at random, so there needs to be a 0 element.

How does this help you work with lists? Simple: every time you say to yourself, "I want the third animal," you translate this "ordinal" number to a "cardinal" number by subtracting 1. The "third" animal is at index 2 and is the penguin. You have to do this because you have spent your whole life using ordinal numbers, and now you have to think in cardinal. Just subtract 1 and you're good.

Remember: ordinal == ordered, 1st; cardinal == cards at random, 0.

Let's practice this. Take this list of animals, and follow the exercises where I tell you to write down what animal you get for that ordinal or cardinal number. Remember, if I say "first," "second," then I'm using ordinal, so subtract 1. If I give you cardinal (like "The animal at 1"), then use it directly.

```
animals = ['bear', 'python3.6', 'peacock', 'kangaroo', 'whale', 'platypus']
```

1.   The animal at 1.

2.   The third (3rd) animal.

3.   The first (1st) animal.

4.   The animal at 3.

5.   The fifth (5th) animal.

6.   The animal at 2.

7.   The sixth (6th) animal.

8.   The animal at 4.

For each of these, write out a full sentence of the form: "The first (1st) animal is at 0 and is a bear." Then say it backwards: "The animal at 0 is the 1st animal and is a bear."

Use your Python to check your answers.

Study Drills

1.   With what you know of the difference between these types of numbers, can you explain why the year 2010 in "January 1, 2010," really is 2010 and not 2009? (Hint: you can't pick years at random.)

2.   Write some more lists and work out similar indexes until you can translate them.

3.   Use Python to check your answers.

WARNING! Programmers will tell you to read this guy named *Dijkstra* on this subject. I recommend you avoid his writings on this unless you enjoy being yelled at by someone who stopped programming at the same time programming started.

Branches and Functions

Y ou have learned if-statements, functions, and lists. Now it's time to bend your mind. Type this in, and see if you can figure out what it's doing.

ex35.py

```
1    from sys import exit
2
3    def gold_room():
4        print("This room is full of gold.  How much do you take?")
5
6        choice = input("> ")
7        if "0" in choice or "1" in choice:
8            how_much = int(choice)
9        else:
10           dead("Man, learn to type a number.")
11
12       if how_much < 50:
13           print("Nice, you're not greedy, you win!")
14           exit(0)
15       else:
16           dead("You greedy bastard!")
17
18
19   def bear_room():
20       print("There is a bear here.")
21       print("The bear has a bunch of honey.")
22       print("The fat bear is in front of another door.")
23       print("How are you going to move the bear?")
24       bear_moved = False
25
26       while True:
27           choice = input("> ")
28
29           if choice == "take honey":
30               dead("The bear looks at you then slaps your face off.")
31           elif choice == "taunt bear" and not bear_moved:
32               print("The bear has moved from the door.")
33               print("You can go through it now.")
34               bear_moved = True
35           elif choice == "taunt bear" and bear_moved:
36               dead("The bear gets pissed off and chews your leg off.")
37           elif choice == "open door" and bear_moved:
38               gold_room()
39           else:
40               print("I got no idea what that means.")
41
```

```
42
43    def cthulhu_room():
44        print("Here you see the great evil Cthulhu.")
45        print("He, it, whatever stares at you and you go insane.")
46        print("Do you flee for your life or eat your head?")
47
48        choice = input("> ")
49
50        if "flee" in choice:
51            start()
52        elif "head" in choice:
53            dead("Well that was tasty!")
54        else:
55            cthulhu_room()
56
57
58    def dead(why):
59        print(why, "Good job!")
60        exit(0)
61
62    def start():
63        print("You are in a dark room.")
64        print("There is a door to your right and left.")
65        print("Which one do you take?")
66
67        choice = input("> ")
68
69        if choice == "left":
70            bear_room()
71        elif choice == "right":
72            cthulhu_room()
73        else:
74            dead("You stumble around the room until you starve.")
75
76
77    start()
```

What You Should See

Here's me playing the game:

```
$ python3.6 ex35.py
You are in a dark room.
There is a door to your right and left.
Which one do you take?
> left
There is a bear here.
The bear has a bunch of honey.
The fat bear is in front of another door.
```

```
How are you going to move the bear?
>  taunt bear
The bear has moved from the door.
You can go through it now.
>  open door
This room is full of gold.  How much do you take?
>  1000
You greedy bastard! Good job!
```

Study Drills

1. Draw a map of the game and how you flow through it.

2. Fix all of your mistakes, including spelling mistakes.

3. Write comments for the functions you do not understand.

4. Add more to the game. What can you do to both simplify and expand it?

5. The gold_ room has a weird way of getting you to type a number. What are all the bugs in this way of doing it? Can you make it better than what I've written? Look at how int() works for clues.

Common Student Questions

Help! How does this program work?!   When you get stuck understanding a piece of code, simply write an English comment above *every* line explaining what that line does. Keep your comments short and similar to the code. Then either diagram how the code works or write a paragraph describing it. If you do that you'll get it.

Why did you write while True?   That makes an infinite loop.

What does exit(0) **do?**   On many operating systems a program can abort with exit(0), and the number passed in will indicate an error or not. If you do exit(1) then it will be an error, but exit(0) will be a good exit. The reason it's backward from normal Boolean logic (with 0==False) is that you can use different numbers to indicate different error results. You can do exit(100) for a different error result than exit(2) or exit(1).

Why is input() **sometimes written as** input('> ')?   The parameter to input is a string that it should print as a prompt before getting the user's input.

Designing and Debugging

N ow that you know if-statements, I'm going to give you some rules for for-loops and while-loops that will keep you out of trouble. I'm also going to give you some tips on debugging so that you can figure out problems with your program. Finally, you will design a little game similar to the last exercise but with a slight twist.

Rules for if-statements

1. Every if-statement must have an else.

2. If this else should never run because it doesn't make sense, then you must use a die function in the else that prints out an error message and dies, just like we did in the last exercise. This will find *many* errors.

3. Never nest if-statements more than two deep and always try to do them one deep.

4. Treat if-statements like paragraphs, where each if-elif-else grouping is like a set of sentences. Put blank lines before and after.

5. Your Boolean tests should be simple. If they are complex, move their calculations to variables earlier in your function and use a good name for the variable.

If you follow these simple rules, you will start writing better code than most programmers. Go back to the last exercise and see if I followed all of these rules. If not, fix my mistakes.

WARNING! Never be a slave to the rules in real life. For training purposes you need to follow these rules to make your mind strong, but in real life sometimes these rules are just stupid. If you think a rule is stupid, try not using it.

Rules for Loops

1. Use a while-loop only to loop forever, and that means probably never. This only applies to Python; other languages are different.

2. Use a for-loop for all other kinds of looping, especially if there is a fixed or limited number of things to loop over.

Tips for Debugging

1. Do not use a "debugger." A debugger is like doing a full-body scan on a sick person. You do not get any specific useful information, and you find a whole lot of information that doesn't help and is just confusing.

2. The best way to debug a program is to use `print` to print out the values of variables at points in the program to see where they go wrong.

3. Make sure parts of your programs work as you work on them. Do not write massive files of code before you try to run them. Code a little, run a little, fix a little.

Homework

Now write a game similar to the one that I created in the last exercise. It can be any kind of game you want in the same flavor. Spend a week on it making it as interesting as possible. For Study Drills, use lists, functions, and modules (remember those from Exercise 13?) as much as possible, and find as many new pieces of Python as you can to make the game work.

Before you start coding you must draw a map for your game. Create the rooms, monsters, and traps that the player must go through on paper before you code.

Once you have your map, try to code it up. If you find problems with the map then adjust it and make the code match.

The best way to work on a piece of software is in small chunks like this:

1. On a sheet of paper or an index card, write a list of tasks you need to complete to finish the software. This is your to-do list.

2. Pick the easiest thing you can do from your list.

3. Write out English comments in your source file as a guide for how you would accomplish this task in your code.

4. Write some of the code under the English comments.

5. Quickly run your script so see if that code worked.

6. Keep working in a cycle of writing some code, running it to test it, and fixing it until it works.

7. Cross this task off your list, then pick your next easiest task and repeat.

This process will help you work on software in a methodical and consistent manner. As you work, update your list by removing tasks you don't really need and adding ones you do.

Symbol Review

It's time to review the symbols and Python words you know and pick up a few more for the next few lessons. I have written out all the Python symbols and keywords that are important to know.

In this lesson take each keyword and first try to write out what it does from memory. Next, search online for it and see what it really does. This may be difficult because some of these are difficult to search for, but try anyway.

If you get one of these wrong from memory, make an index card with the correct definition and try to "correct" your memory.

Finally, use each of these in a small Python program, or as many as you can get done. The goal is to find out what the symbol does, make sure you got it right, correct it if you did not, then use it to lock it in.

Keywords

Keyword	Description	Example
and	Logical and.	`True and False == False`
as	Part of the `with-as` statement.	`with X as Y: pass`
assert	Assert (ensure) that something is true.	`assert False, "Error!"`
break	Stop this loop right now.	`while True: break`
class	Define a class.	`class Person(object)`
continue	Don't process more of the loop, do it again.	`while True: continue`
def	Define a function.	`def X(): pass`
del	Delete from dictionary.	`del X[Y]`
elif	Else if condition.	`if: X; elif: Y; else: J`
else	Else condition.	`if: X; elif: Y; else: J`
except	If an exception happens, do this.	`except ValueError as e: print(e)`
exec	Run a string as Python.	`exec 'print("hello")'`
finally	Exceptions or not, finally do this no matter what.	`finally: pass`
for	Loop over a collection of things.	`for X in Y: pass`
from	Import specific parts of a module.	`from x import Y`
global	Declare that you want a global variable.	`global X`

Keyword	Description	Example
`if`	If condition.	`if: X; elif: Y; else: J`
`import`	Import a module into this one to use.	`import os`
`in`	Part of `for-loops`. Also a test of X in Y.	`for X in Y: pass` also `1 in [1] == True`
`is`	Like == to test equality.	`1 is 1 == True`
`lambda`	Create a short anonymous function.	`s = lambda y: y ** y; s(3)`
`not`	Logical not.	`not True == False`
`or`	Logical or.	`True or False == True`
`pass`	This block is empty.	`def empty(): pass`
`print`	Print this string.	`print('this string')`
`raise`	Raise an exception when things go wrong.	`raise ValueError("No")`
`return`	Exit the function with a return value.	`def X(): return Y`
`try`	Try this block, and if exception, go to except.	`try: pass`
`while`	While loop.	`while X: pass`
`with`	With an expression as a variable do.	`with X as Y: pass`
`yield`	Pause here and return to caller.	`def X(): yield Y; X().next()`

Data Types

For data types, write out what makes up each one. For example, with strings, write out how you create a string. For numbers, write out a few numbers.

Type	Description	Example
`True`	True Boolean value.	`True or False == True`
`False`	False Boolean value.	`False and True == False`
`None`	Represents "nothing" or "no value."	`x = None`
`bytes`	Stores bytes, maybe of text, PNG, file, etc.	`x = b"hello"`
`strings`	Stores textual information.	`x = "hello"`
`numbers`	Stores integers.	`i = 100`
`floats`	Stores decimals.	`i = 10.389`
`lists`	Stores a list of things.	`j = [1,2,3,4]`
`dicts`	Stores a key=value mapping of things.	`e = {'x': 1, 'y': 2}`

String Escape Sequences

For string escape sequences, use them in strings to make sure they do what you think they do.

Escape	Description
\\	Backslash
\'	Single-quote
\"	Double-quote
\a	Bell
\b	Backspace
\f	Formfeed
\n	Newline
\r	Carriage
\t	Tab
\v	Vertical tab

Old Style String Formats

Same thing for string formats: use them in some strings to know what they do. Older Python 2 code uses these formatting characters to do what f-strings do. Try them out as an alternative.

Escape	Description	Example
%d	Decimal integers (not floating point)	"%d" % 45 == '45'
%i	Same as %d	"%i" % 45 == '45'
%o	Octal number	"%o" % 1000 == '1750'
%u	Unsigned decimal	"%u" % -1000 == '-1000'
%x	Hexadecimal lowercase	"%x" % 1000 == '3e8'
%X	Hexadecimal uppercase	"%X" % 1000 == '3E8'
%e	Exponential notation, lowercase "e"	"%e" % 1000 == '1.000000e+03'
%E	Exponential notation, uppercase "E"	"%E" % 1000 == '1.000000E+03'
%f	Floating point real number	"%f" % 10.34 == '10.340000'
%F	Same as %f	"%F" % 10.34 == '10.340000'
%g	Either %f or %e, whichever is shorter	"%g" % 10.34 == '10.34'
%G	Same as %g but uppercase	"%G" % 10.34 == '10.34'
%c	Character format	"%c" % 34 == '"'
%r	Repr format (debugging format)	"%r" % int == "<type 'int'>"
%s	String format	"%s there" % 'hi' == 'hi there'
%%	A percent sign	"%g%%" % 10.34 == '10.34%'

Operators

Some of these may be unfamiliar to you, but look them up anyway. Find out what they do, and if you still can't figure it out, save it for later.

Operator	Description	Example
+	Addition	`2 + 4 == 6`
-	Subtraction	`2 - 4 == -2`
*	Multiplication	`2 * 4 == 8`
**	Power of	`2 ** 4 == 16`
/	Division	`2 / 4 == 0.5`
//	Floor division	`2 // 4 == 0`
%	String interpolate or modulus	`2 % 4 == 2`
<	Less than	`4 < 4 == False`
>	Greater than	`4 > 4 == False`
<=	Less than equal	`4 <= 4 == True`
>=	Greater than equal	`4 >= 4 == True`
==	Equal	`4 == 5 == False`
!=	Not equal	`4 != 5 == True`
( )	Parentheses	`len('hi') == 2`
[ ]	List brackets	`[1,3,4]`
{ }	Dict curly braces	`{'x': 5, 'y': 10}`
@	At (decorators)	`@classmethod`
,	Comma	`range(0, 10)`
:	Colon	`def X():`
.	Dot	`self.x = 10`
=	Assign equal	`x = 10`
;	Semi-colon	`print("hi");` `print("there")`
+=	Add and assign	`x = 1; x += 2`
-=	Subtract and assign	`x = 1; x -= 2`
*=	Multiply and assign	`x = 1; x *= 2`
/=	Divide and assign	`x = 1; x /= 2`
//=	Floor divide and assign	`x = 1; x //= 2`
%=	Modulus assign	`x = 1; x %= 2`
**=	Power assign	`x = 1; x **= 2`

Spend about a week on this, but if you finish faster that's great. The point is to try to get coverage on all these symbols and make sure they are locked in your head. What's also important is to find out what you *do not* know so you can fix it later.

Reading Code

Now find some Python code to read. You should be reading any Python code you can and trying to steal ideas that you find. You actually should have enough knowledge to be able to read but maybe not understand what the code does. What this lesson teaches is how to apply things you have learned to understand other people's code.

First, print out the code you want to understand. Yes, print it out, because your eyes and brain are more used to reading paper than computer screens. Make sure you print a few pages at a time.

Second, go through your printout and take notes on the following:

1. Functions and what they do.
2. Where each variable is first given a value.
3. Any variables with the same names in different parts of the program. These may be trouble later.
4. Any if-statements without else clauses. Are they right?
5. Any while-loops that might not end.
6. Any parts of code that you can't understand for whatever reason.

Third, once you have all of this marked up, try to explain it to yourself by writing comments as you go. Explain the functions, how they are used, what variables are involved, and anything you can to figure this code out.

Last, on all of the difficult parts, trace the values of each variable line by line, function by function. In fact, do another printout, and write in the margin the value of each variable that you need to "trace."

Once you have a good idea of what the code does, go back to the computer and read it again to see if you find new things. Keep finding more code and doing this until you do not need the printouts anymore.

Study Drills

1. Find out what a "flow chart" is and draw a few.

2. If you find errors in code you are reading, try to fix them, and send the author your changes.

3. Another technique for when you are not using paper is to put comments with your notes in the code. Sometimes, these could become the actual comments to help the next person.

Common Student Questions

How would I search for these things online?   Simply put "python3.6" before anything you want to find. For example, to find "yield" search for "python3.6 yield."

Doing Things to Lists

Y ou have learned about lists. When you learned about while-loops you "appended" numbers to the end of a list and printed them out. There were also Study Drills where you were supposed to find all the other things you can do to lists in the Python documentation. That was a while back, so review those topics if you do not know what I'm talking about.

Found it? Remember it? Good. When you did this you had a list, and you "called" the function append on it. However, you may not really understand what's going on so let's see what we can do to lists.

When you write mystuff.append('hello') you are actually setting off a chain of events inside Python to cause something to happen to the mystuff list. Here's how it works:

1. Python sees you mentioned mystuff and looks up that variable. It might have to look backward to see if you created it with =, if it is a function argument, or if it's a global variable. Either way, it has to find mystuff first.

2. Once it finds mystuff it reads the . (period) operator and starts to look at *variables* that are a part of mystuff. Since mystuff is a list, it knows that mystuff has a bunch of functions.

3. It then hits append and compares the name to all the names that mystuff says it owns. If append is in there (it is), then Python grabs *that* to use.

4. Next Python sees the ((open parenthesis) and realizes, "Oh hey, this should be a function." At this point it *calls* (runs or executes) the function just like normal, but it calls the function with an *extra* argument.

5. That *extra* argument is ... mystuff! I know, weird, right? But that's how Python works, so it's best to just remember it and assume that's the result. What happens, at the end of all this, is a function call that looks like append(mystuff, 'hello') instead of what you read, which is mystuff.append('hello').

For the most part you do not have to know that this is going on, but it helps when you get error messages from Python like this:

```
$ python3.6
>>> class Thing(object):
...     def test(message):
...             print(message)
...
>>> a = Thing()
>>> a.test("hello")
```

```
Traceback (most recent call last):
  File "<stdin>", line 1, in <module>
TypeError: test() takes exactly 1 argument (2 given)
>>>
```

What was all that? Well, this is me typing into the Python shell and showing you some magic. You haven't seen class yet, but we'll get into that later. For now you see how Python said test() takes exactly 1 argument (2 given). If you see this, it means that Python changed a.test("hello") to test(a, "hello") and that somewhere someone messed up and didn't add the argument for a.

This might be a lot to take in, but we're going to spend a few exercises getting this concept firm in your brain. To kick things off, here's an exercise that mixes strings and lists for all kinds of fun.

ex38.py

```
1  ten_things = "Apples Oranges Crows Telephone Light Sugar"
2
3  print("Wait there are not 10 things in that list. Let's fix that.")
4
5  stuff = ten_things.split(' ')
6  more_stuff = ["Day", "Night", "Song", "Frisbee",
7                "Corn", "Banana", "Girl", "Boy"]
8
9  while len(stuff) != 10:
10     next_one = more_stuff.pop()
11     print("Adding: ", next_one)
12     stuff.append(next_one)
13     print(f"There are {len(stuff)} items now.")
14
15 print("There we go: ", stuff)
16
17 print("Let's do some things with stuff.")
18
19 print(stuff[1])
20 print(stuff[-1]) # whoa! fancy
21 print(stuff.pop())
22 print(' '.join(stuff)) # what? cool!
23 print('#'.join(stuff[3:5])) # super stellar!
```

What You Should See

```
Wait there are not 10 things in that list. Let's fix that.
Adding:  Boy
There are 7 items now.
Adding:  Girl
There are 8 items now.
Adding:  Banana
There are 9 items now.
```

```
Adding:  Corn
There are 10 items now.
There we go:  ['Apples', 'Oranges', 'Crows', 'Telephone', 'Light',
     'Sugar', 'Boy', 'Girl', 'Banana', 'Corn']
Let's do some things with stuff.
Oranges
Corn
Corn
Apples Oranges Crows Telephone Light Sugar Boy Girl Banana
Telephone#Light
```

What Lists Can Do

Let's say you want to create a computer game based on *Go Fish*. If you don't know what *Go Fish* is, take the time now to go read up on it on the internet. To do this you would need to have some way of taking the concept of a "deck of cards" and putting it into your Python program. You then have to write Python code that knows how to work this imaginary version of a deck of cards so that a person playing your game thinks that it's real, even if it isn't. What you need is a "deck of cards" structure, and programmers call this kind of thing a *data structure*.

What's a data structure? If you think about it, a *data structure* is just a formal way to *structure* (organize) some *data* (facts). It really is that simple. Even though some data structures can get insanely complex, all they are is just a way to store facts inside a program so you can access them in different ways. They structure data.

I'll be getting into this more in the next exercise, but lists are one of the most common data structures programmers use. A list is an ordered list of things you want to store and access randomly or linearly by an index. What?! Remember what I said though: just because a programmer said "list is a list" doesn't mean that it's any more complex than what a list already is in the real world. Let's look at the deck of cards as an example of a list:

1. You have a bunch of cards with values.

2. Those cards are in a stack, list, or list from the top card to the bottom card.

3. You can take cards off the top, the bottom, or the middle at random.

4. If you want to find a specific card, you have to grab the deck and go through it one at a time.

Let's look at what I said:

"An ordered list"   Yes, deck of cards is in order with a first and a last.

"of things you want to store"   Yes, cards are things I want to store.

"and access randomly"   Yes, I can grab a card from anywhere in the deck.

"or linearly"   Yes, if I want to find a specific card I can start at the beginning and go in order.

"by an index"   Almost, since with a deck of cards if I told you to get the card at index 19 you'd have to count until you found that one. In our Python lists the computer can just jump right to any index you give it.

That is all a list does, and this should give you a way to figure out concepts in programming. Every concept in programming usually has some relationship to the real world. At least, the useful ones do. If you can figure out what the analog in the real world is, then you can use that to figure out what the data structure should be able to do.

When to Use Lists

You use a list whenever you have something that matches the list data structure's useful features:

1. If you need to maintain order. Remember, this is listed order, not *sorted* order. Lists do not sort for you.

2. If you need to access the contents randomly by a number. Remember, this is using *cardinal* numbers starting at 0.

3. If you need to go through the contents linearly (first to last). Remember, that's what `for-loops` are for.

This is when you use a list.

Study Drills

1. Take each function that is called, and go through the steps for function calls to translate them to what Python does. For example, `more_stuff.pop()` is `pop(more_stuff)`.

2. Translate these two ways to view the function calls in English. For example, `more_stuff.pop()` reads as, "Call `pop` on `more_stuff`." Meanwhile, `pop(more_stuff)` means, "Call `pop` with argument `more_stuff`." Understand how they are really the same thing.

3. Go read about object-oriented programming online. Confused? I was, too. Do not worry. You will learn enough to be dangerous, and you can slowly learn more later.

4. Read up on what a class is in Python. *Do not read about how other languages use the word "class."* That will only mess you up.

5. Do not worry If you do not have any idea what I'm talking about. Programmers like to feel smart, so they invented object-oriented programming, named it OOP, and then used it way too much. If you think that's hard, you should try to use "functional programming."

6. Find 10 examples of things in the real world that would fit in a list. Try writing some scripts to work with them.

Common Student Questions

Didn't you say to not use `while-loops`? Yes, so just remember sometimes you can break the rules if you have a good reason. Only idiots are slaves to rules all the time.

Why does `join(' ', stuff)` **not work?** The way the documentation for `join` is written doesn't make sense. It does not work like that and is instead a method you call on the *inserted* string to put between the list to be joined. Rewrite it like `' '.join(stuff)`.

Why did you use a `while-loop`? Try rewriting it with a `for-loop` and see if that's easier.

What does `stuff[3:5]` **do?** That extracts a "slice" from the `stuff` list that is from element 3 to element 4, meaning it does *not* include element 5. It's similar to how `range(3,5)` would work.

Dictionaries, Oh Lovely Dictionaries

Y ou are now going to learn about the Dictionary data structure in Python. A Dictionary (or *dict*) is a way to store data just like a list, but instead of using only numbers to get the data, you can use almost anything. This lets you treat a dict like it's a database for storing and organizing data.

Let's compare what dicts can do to what lists can do. You see, a list lets you do this:

Exercise 39 Python Session

```
>>> things = ['a', 'b', 'c', 'd']
>>> print(things[1])
b
>>> things[1] = 'z'
>>> print(things[1])
z
>>> things
['a', 'z', 'c', 'd']
```

You can use numbers to *index* into a list, meaning you can use numbers to find out what's in lists. You should know this about lists by now, but make sure you understand that you can *only* use numbers to get items out of a list.

A dict lets you use *anything*, not just numbers. Yes, a dict associates one thing to another, no matter what it is. Take a look:

Exercise 39 Python Session

```
>>> stuff = {'name': 'Zed', 'age': 39, 'height': 6 * 12 + 2}
>>> print(stuff['name'])
Zed
>>> print(stuff['age'])
39
>>> print(stuff['height'])
74
>>> stuff['city'] = "SF"
>>> print(stuff['city'])
SF
```

You will see that instead of just numbers we're using strings to say what we want from the stuff dictionary. We can also put new things into the dictionary with strings. It doesn't have to be strings, though. We can also do this:

Exercise 39 Python Session

```
>>> stuff[1] = "Wow"
>>> stuff[2] = "Neato"
>>> print(stuff[1])
```

```
Wow
>>> print(stuff[2])
Neato
```

In this code I used numbers, and then you can see there are numbers and strings as keys in the dict when I print it. I could use anything. Well almost, but just pretend you can use anything for now.

Of course, a dictionary that you can only put things in is pretty stupid, so here's how you delete things, with the del keyword:

Exercise 39 Python Session

```
>>> del stuff['city']
>>> del stuff[1]
>>> del stuff[2]
>>> stuff
{'name': 'Zed', 'age': 39, 'height': 74}
```

A Dictionary Example

We'll now do an exercise that you *must* study very carefully. I want you to type this code in and try to understand what's going on. Take note of when you put things in a dict, get them from a hash, and all the operations you use. Notice how this example is mapping states to their abbreviations and then the abbreviations to cities in the states. Remember, *mapping* (or *associating*) is the key concept in a dictionary.

ex39.py

```
1    # create a mapping of state to abbreviation
2    states = {
3        'Oregon': 'OR',
4        'Florida': 'FL',
5        'California': 'CA',
6        'New York': 'NY',
7        'Michigan': 'MI'
8    }
9
10   # create a basic set of states and some cities in them
11   cities = {
12       'CA': 'San Francisco',
13       'MI': 'Detroit',
14       'FL': 'Jacksonville'
15   }
16
17   # add some more cities
18   cities['NY'] = 'New York'
19   cities['OR'] = 'Portland'
20
21   # print out some cities
22   print('-' * 10)
```

```
23    print("NY State has: ", cities['NY'])
24    print("OR State has: ", cities['OR'])
25
26    # print some states
27    print('-' * 10)
28    print("Michigan's abbreviation is: ", states['Michigan'])
29    print("Florida's abbreviation is: ", states['Florida'])
30
31    # do it by using the state then cities dict
32    print('-' * 10)
33    print("Michigan has: ", cities[states['Michigan']])
34    print("Florida has: ", cities[states['Florida']])
35
36    # print every state abbreviation
37    print('-' * 10)
38    for state, abbrev in list(states.items()):
39        print(f"{state} is abbreviated {abbrev}")
40
41    # print every city in state
42    print('-' * 10)
43    for abbrev, city in list(cities.items()):
44        print(f"{abbrev} has the city {city}")
45
46    # now do both at the same time
47    print('-' * 10)
48    for state, abbrev in list(states.items()):
49        print(f"{state} state is abbreviated {abbrev}')
50        print(f"and has city {cities[abbrev]}")
51
52    print('-' * 10)
53    # safely get a abbreviation by state that might not be there
54    state = states.get('Texas')
55
56    if not state:
57        print("Sorry, no Texas.")
58
59    # get a city with a default value
60    city = cities.get('TX', 'Does Not Exist')
61    print(f"The city for the state 'TX' is: {city}")
```

What You Should See

```
$ python3.6 ex39.py
----------
NY State has:  New York
OR State has:  Portland
----------
Michigan's abbreviation is:  MI
Florida's abbreviation is:  FL
```

```
----------
Michigan has:  Detroit
Florida has:  Jacksonville
----------
Oregon is abbreviated OR
Florida is abbreviated FL
California is abbreviated CA
New York is abbreviated NY
Michigan is abbreviated MI
----------
CA has the city San Francisco
MI has the city Detroit
FL has the city Jacksonville
NY has the city New York
OR has the city Portland
----------
Oregon state is abbreviated OR
and has city Portland
Florida state is abbreviated FL
and has city Jacksonville
California state is abbreviated CA
and has city San Francisco
New York state is abbreviated NY
and has city New York
Michigan state is abbreviated MI
and has city Detroit
----------
Sorry, no Texas.
The city for the state 'TX' is: Does Not Exist
```

What Dictionaries Can Do

A dictionary is another example of a data structure, and, like a list, it is one of the most commonly used data structures in programming. A dictionary is used to *map* or *associate* things you want to store to keys you need to get them. Again, programmers don't use a term like "dictionary" for something that doesn't work like an actual dictionary full of words, so let's use that as our real world example.

Let's say you want to find out what the word "honorificabilitudinitatibus" means. Today you would simply copy-paste that word into a search engine and then find out the answer, and we could say a search engine is like a really huge super complex version of the *Oxford English Dictionary* (OED). Before search engines what you would do is this:

1. Go to your library and get "the dictionary." Let's say it's the OED.

2. You know "honorificabilitudinitatibus" starts with the letter "H" so you look on the side of the book for the little tab that has "H" on it.

3. Skim the pages until you are close to where "hon" starts.

4.   Skim a few more pages until you find "honorificabilitudinitatibus" or hit the beginning of the "hp" words and realize this word isn't in the OED.

5.   Once you find the entry, you read the definition to figure out what it means.

This process is nearly exactly the way a dict works, and you are basically "mapping" the word "honorificabilitudinitatibus" to its definition. A dict in Python is just like a dictionary in the real world such as the OED.

Study Drills

1.   Do this same kind of mapping with cities and states/regions in your country or some other country.

2.   Find the Python documentation for dictionaries and try to do even more things to them.

3.   Find out what you *can't* do with dictionaries. A big one is that they do not have order, so try playing with that.

Common Student Questions

What is the difference between a list and a dictionary?   A list is for an ordered list of items. A dictionary (or dict) is for matching some items (called "keys") to other items (called "values").

What would I use a dictionary for?   When you have to take one value and "look up" another value. In fact, you could call dictionaries "look up tables."

What would I use a list for?   Use a list for any sequence of things that needs to be in order, and you only need to look them up by a numeric index.

What if I need a dictionary, but I need it to be in order?   Take   a   look   at   the   `collections` `.OrderedDict` data structure in Python. Search for it online to find the documentation.

Modules, Classes, and Objects

Python is called an "object-oriented programming language." This means there is a construct in Python called a *class* that lets you structure your software in a particular way. Using classes, you can add consistency to your programs so that they can be used in a cleaner way. At least that's the theory.

I am now going to teach you the beginnings of object-oriented programming, classes, and objects using what you already know about dictionaries and modules. My problem is that object-oriented programming (OOP) is just plain weird. You have to struggle with this, try to understand what I say here, type in the code, and in the next exercise I'll hammer it in.

Here we go.

Modules Are Like Dictionaries

You know how a dictionary is created and used and that it is a way to map one thing to another. That means if you have a dictionary with a key "apple" and you want to get it then you do this:

ex40a.py

```
1    mystuff = {'apple': "I AM APPLES!"}
2    print(mystuff['apple'])
```

Keep this idea of "get X from Y" in your head, and now think about modules. You've made a few so far, and you should know they are:

1. A Python file with some functions or variables in it . . .

2. Which you can import . . .

3. And access the functions or variables of with the . (dot) operator.

Imagine I have a module that I decide to name `mystuff.py` and I put a function in it called `apple`. Here's the module `mystuff.py`:

ex40a.py

```
1    # this goes in mystuff.py
2    def apple():
3        print("I AM APPLES!")
```

Once I have this code, I can use the module `MyStuff` with `import` and then access the `apple` function:

ex40a.py

```
1    import mystuff
2    mystuff.apple()
```

I could also put a variable in it named `tangerine`:

ex40a.py

```
1    def apple():
2        print("I AM APPLES!")
3
4    # this is just a variable
5    tangerine = "Living reflection of a dream"
```

I can access that the same way:

ex40a.py

```
1    import mystuff
2
3    mystuff.apple()
4    print(mystuff.tangerine)
```

Refer back to the dictionary, and you should start to see how this is similar to using a dictionary, but the syntax is different. Let's compare:

ex40a.py

```
1    mystuff['apple'] # get apple from dict
2    mystuff.apple() # get apple from the module
3    mystuff.tangerine # same thing, it's just a variable
```

This means we have a *very* common pattern in Python:

1. Take a key=value style container.

2. Get something out of it by the key's name.

In the case of the dictionary, the key is a string and the syntax is `[key]`. In the case of the module, the key is an identifier, and the syntax is `.key`. Other than that they are nearly the same thing.

Classes Are Like Modules

You can think about a module as a specialized dictionary that can store Python code so you can access it with the `.` operator. Python also has another construct that serves a similar purpose called a class. A class is a way to take a grouping of functions and data and place them inside a container so you can access them with the `.` (dot) operator.

If I were to create a class just like the `mystuff` module, I'd do something like this:

```
1    class MyStuff(object):
2
3        def __init__(self):
4            self.tangerine = "And now a thousand years between"
5
6        def apple(self):
7            print("I AM CLASSY APPLES!")
```

That looks complicated compared to modules, and there is definitely a lot going on by comparison, but you should be able to make out how this is like a "mini-module" with `MyStuff` having an `apple()` function in it. What is probably confusing is the `__init__()` function and use of `self.tangerine` for setting the `tangerine` instance variable.

Here's why classes are used instead of modules: You can take this `MyStuff` class and use it to craft many of them, millions at a time if you want, and each one won't interfere with each other. When you import a module there is only one for the entire program unless you do some monster hacks.

Before you can understand this, though, you need to know what an "object" is and how to work with `MyStuff` just like you do with the `mystuff.py` module.

Objects Are Like Import

If a class is like a "mini-module," then there has to be a concept similar to `import` but for classes. That concept is called "instantiate," which is just a fancy, obnoxious, overly smart way to say "create." When you instantiate a class what you get is called an object.

You instantiate (create) a class by calling the class like it's a function, like this:

```
1    thing = MyStuff()
2    thing.apple()
3    print(thing.tangerine)
```

The first line is the "instantiate" operation, and it's a lot like calling a function. However, Python coordinates a sequence of events for you behind the scenes. I'll go through these steps using the preceding code for `MyStuff`:

1.   Python looks for `MyStuff()` and sees that it is a class you've defined.

2.   Python crafts an empty object with all the functions you've specified in the class using `def`.

3. Python then looks to see if you made a "magic" __init__ function, and if you have it calls that function to initialize your newly created empty object.

4. In the `MyStuff` function __init__ you then get this extra variable, `self`, which is that empty object Python made for you, and you can set variables on it just like you would with a module, dictionary, or other object.

5. In this case, you set `self.tangerine` to a song lyric and then you've initialized this object.

6. Now Python can take this newly minted object and assign it to the `thing` variable for you to work with.

That's the basics of how Python does this "mini-import" when you call a class like a function. Remember that this is *not* giving you the class but instead is using the class as a *blueprint* for building a copy of that type of thing.

Keep in mind that I'm giving you a slightly inaccurate idea of how these work so that you can start to build up an understanding of classes based on what you know about modules. The truth is, classes and objects suddenly diverge from modules at this point. If I were being totally honest, I'd say something more like this:

- Classes are like blueprints or definitions for creating new mini-modules.

- Instantiation is how you make one of these mini-modules *and* import it at the same time. "Instantiate" just means to create an object from the class.

- The resulting created mini-module is called an object, and you then assign it to a variable to work with it.

At this point objects behave differently from modules, and this should only serve as a way for you to bridge over to understanding classes and objects.

Getting Things from Things

I now have three ways to get things from things:

ex40a.py

```
1    # dict style
2    mystuff['apples']
3
4    # module style
5    mystuff.apples()
6    print(mystuff.tangerine)
7
8    # class style
9    thing = MyStuff()
10   thing.apples()
11   print(thing.tangerine)
```

A First Class Example

You should start seeing the similarities in these three key=value container types and probably have a bunch of questions. Hang on with the questions, as the next exercise will hammer home your "object-oriented vocabulary." In this exercise, I just want you to type in this code and get it working so that you have some experience before moving on.

ex40.py

```
 1   class Song(object):
 2
 3       def __init__(self, lyrics):
 4           self.lyrics = lyrics
 5
 6       def sing_me_a_song(self):
 7           for line in self.lyrics:
 8               print(line)
 9
10   happy_bday = Song(["Happy birthday to you",
11                      "I don't want to get sued",
12                      "So I'll stop right there"])
13
14   bulls_on_parade = Song(["They rally around tha family",
15                           "With pockets full of shells"])
16
17   happy_bday.sing_me_a_song()
18
19   bulls_on_parade.sing_me_a_song()
```

What You Should See

Exercise 40 Session

```
$ python3.6 ex40.py
Happy birthday to you
I don't want to get sued
So I'll stop right there
They rally around tha family
With pockets full of shells
```

Study Drills

1. Write some more songs using this and make sure you understand that you're passing a list of strings as the lyrics.
2. Put the lyrics in a separate variable, then pass that variable to the class to use instead.

3. See if you can hack on this and make it do more things. Don't worry if you have no idea how, just give it a try, and see what happens. Break it, trash it, thrash it, you can't hurt it.

4. Search online for "object-oriented programming" and try to overflow your brain with what you read. Don't worry if it makes absolutely no sense to you. Half of that stuff makes no sense to me, too.

Common Student Questions

Why do I need `self` **when I make** `__init__` **or other functions for classes?** If you don't have `self`, then code like `cheese = 'Frank'` is ambiguous. That code isn't clear about whether you mean the *instance's* cheese attribute *or* a local variable named `cheese`. With `self.cheese = 'Frank'` it's very clear you mean the instance attribute `self.cheese`.

Learning to Speak Object-Oriented

In this exercise I'm going to teach you how to speak "object-oriented." What I'll do is give you a small set of words with definitions you need to know. Then I'll give you a set of sentences with holes in them that you'll have to understand. Finally, I'm going to give you a large set of exercises that you have to complete to make these sentences solid in your vocabulary.

Word Drills

class   Tell Python to make a new type of thing.

object   Two meanings: the most basic type of thing, and any instance of some thing.

instance   What you get when you tell Python to create a class.

def   How you define a function inside a class.

self   Inside the functions in a class, self is a variable for the instance/object being accessed.

inheritance   The concept that one class can inherit traits from another class, much like you and your parents.

composition   The concept that a class can be composed of other classes as parts, much like how a car has wheels.

attribute   A property classes have that are from composition and are usually variables.

is-a   A phrase to say that something inherits from another, as in a "salmon" is-a "fish."

has-a   A phrase to say that something is composed of other things or has a trait, as in "a salmon has-a mouth."

Take some time to make flash cards for these terms and memorize them. As usual, this won't make too much sense until after you are finished with this exercise, but you need to know the base words first.

Phrase Drills

Next I have a list of Python code snippets on the left, and the English sentences for them:

class X(Y)   "Make a class named X that is-a Y."

class X(object): def __init__(self, J)   "class X has-a __init__ that takes self and J parameters."

class X(object): def M(self, J)   "class X has-a function named M that takes self and J parameters."

foo = X()   "Set foo to an instance of class X."

foo.M(J)   "From foo, get the M function, and call it with parameters self, J."

foo.K = Q   "From foo, get the K attribute, and set it to Q."

In each of these, where you see X, Y, M, J, K, Q, and foo, you can treat those like blank spots. For example, I can also write these sentences as follows:

1. "Make a class named ??? that is-a Y."
2. "class ??? has-a __init__ that takes self and ??? parameters."
3. "class ??? has-a function named ??? that takes self and ??? parameters."
4. "Set ??? to an instance of class ???."
5. "From ???, get the ??? function, and call it with self=??? and parameters ???."
6. "From ???, get the ??? attribute, and set it to ???."

Again, write these on some flash cards and drill them. Put the Python code snippet on the front and the sentence on the back. You *have* to be able to say the sentence exactly the same every time whenever you see that form. Not sort of the same, but exactly the same.

Combined Drills

The final preparation for you is to combine the words drills with the phrase drills. What I want you to do for this drill is this:

1. Take a phrase card and drill it.
2. Flip it over and read the sentence, and for each word in the sentence that is in your words drills, get that card.
3. Drill those words for that sentence.
4. Keep going until you are bored, then take a break and do it again.

A Reading Test

I now have a little Python hack script that will drill you on these words you know in an infinite manner. This is a simple script you should be able to figure out, and the only thing it does is use a library called urllib to download a list of words I have. Here's the script, which you should enter into oop_test.py to work with it:

ex41.py

```
1   import random
2   from urllib.request import urlopen
3   import sys
4
```

```
5    WORD_URL = "http://learncodethehardway.org/words.txt"
6    WORDS = []
7
8    PHRASES = {
9        "class %%%(%%%):":
10           "Make a class named %%% that is-a %%%.",
11       "class %%%(object):\n\tdef __init__(self, ***)" :
12           "class %%% has-a __init__ that takes self and *** params.",
13       "class %%%(object):\n\tdef ***(self, @@@)":
14           "class %%% has-a function *** that takes self and @@@ params.",
15       "*** = %%%()":
16           "Set *** to an instance of class %%%.",
17       "***.***(@@@)":
18           "From *** get the *** function, call it with params self, @@@.",
19       "***.*** = '***'":
20           "From *** get the *** attribute and set it to '***'."
21   }
22
23   # do they want to drill phrases first
24   if len(sys.argv) == 2 and sys.argv[1] == "english":
25       PHRASE_FIRST = True
26   else:
27       PHRASE_FIRST = False
28
29   # load up the words from the website
30   for word in urlopen(WORD_URL).readlines():
31       WORDS.append(str(word.strip(), encoding="utf-8'))
32
33
34   def convert(snippet, phrase):
35       class_names = [w.capitalize() for w in
36                       random.sample(WORDS, snippet.count("%%%"))]
37       other_names = random.sample(WORDS, snippet.count("***"))
38       results = []
39       param_names = []
40
41       for i in range(0, snippet.count("@@@")):
42           param_count = random.randint(1,3)
43           param_names.append(', '.join(
44               random.sample(WORDS, param_count)))
45
46       for sentence in snippet, phrase:
47           result = sentence[:]
48
49           # fake class names
50           for word in class_names:
51               result = result.replace("%%%", word, 1)
52
53           # fake other names
54           for word in other_names:
```

```
55                    result = result.replace("***", word, 1)
56
57            # fake parameter lists
58            for word in param_names:
59                    result = result.replace("@@@", word, 1)
60
61            results.append(result)
62
63        return results
64
65
66    # keep going until they hit CTRL-D
67    try:
68        while True:
69                snippets = list(PHRASES.keys())
70                random.shuffle(snippets)
71
72            for snippet in snippets:
73                phrase = PHRASES[snippet]
74                question, answer = convert(snippet, phrase)
75                if PHRASE_FIRST:
76                    question, answer = answer, question
77
78                print(question)
79
80                input("> ")
81                print(f"ANSWER:  {answer}\n\n")
82    except EOFError:
83        print("\nBye")
```

Run this script and try to translate the "object-oriented phrases" into English translations. You should see that the PHRASES dict has both forms and that you just have to enter the correct one.

Practice English to Code

Next you should run the script with the "english" option so that you drill the inverse operation:

```
$ python oop_test.py english
```

Remember that these phrases are using nonsense words. Part of learning to read code well is to stop placing so much meaning on the names used for variables and classes. Too often people will read a word like "Cork" and suddenly get derailed because that word will confuse them about the meaning. In the above example, "Cork" is just an arbitrary name chosen for a class. Don't place any other meaning on it, and instead treat it like the patterns I've given you.

Reading More Code

You are now to go on a new quest to read even more code, to read the phrases you just learned in the code you read. You will look for all the files with classes and then do the following:

1.   For each class give its name and what other classes it inherits from.

2.   Under that, list every function it has and the parameters they take.

3.   List all of the attributes it uses on its self.

4.   For each attribute, give the class this attribute is.

The goal is to go through real code and start learning to "pattern match" the phrases you just learned against how they're used. If you drill this enough you should start to see these patterns shout at you in the code whereas before they just seemed like vague blank spots you didn't know.

Common Student Questions

What does `result = sentence[:]` **do?**   That's a Python way of copying a list. You're using the list slice syntax `[:]` to effectively make a slice from the very first element to the very last one.

This script is hard to get running!   By this point you should be able to type this in and get it working. It does have a few little tricks here and there, but there's nothing complex about it. Just do all the things you've learned so far to debug scripts. Type each line in, confirm that it's *exactly* like mine, and research anything you don't know online.

It's still too hard!   You can do this. Take it very slow, character by character if you have to, but type it in exactly and figure out what it does.

Is-A, Has-A, Objects, and Classes

An important concept that you have to understand is the difference between a class and an object. The problem is, there is no real "difference" between a class and an object. They are actually the same thing at different points in time. I will demonstrate with a Zen koan:

> What is the difference between a fish and a salmon?

Did that question sort of confuse you? Really sit down and think about it for a minute. I mean, a fish and a salmon are different but, wait, they are the same thing, right? A salmon is a *kind* of fish, so, I mean, it's not different. But at the same time, a salmon is a particular *type* of fish, so it's actually different from all other fish. That's what makes it a salmon and not a halibut. So a salmon and a fish are the same but different. Weird.

This question is confusing because most people do not think about real things this way, but they intuitively understand them. You do not need to think about the difference between a fish and a salmon because you *know* how they are related. You know a salmon is a *kind* of fish and that there are other kinds of fish without having to understand that.

Let's take it one step further. Let's say you have a bucket full of three salmon and because you are a nice person, you have decided to name them Frank, Joe, and Mary. Now, think about this question:

> What is the difference between Mary and a salmon?

Again this is a weird question, but it's a bit easier than the fish versus salmon question. You know that Mary is a salmon, so she's not really different. She's just a specific "instance" of a salmon. Joe and Frank are also instances of salmon. What do I mean when I say instance? I mean they were created from some other salmon and now represent a real thing that has salmon-like attributes.

Now for the mind-bending idea: Fish is a class, and Salmon is a class, and Mary is an object. Think about that for a second. Let's break it down slowly and see if you get it.

A fish is a class, meaning it's not a *real* thing, but rather a word we attach to instances of things with similar attributes. Got fins? Got gills? Lives in water? Alright it's probably a fish.

Someone with a Ph.D. then comes along and says, "No, my young friend, *this* fish is actually *Salmo salar*, affectionately known as a salmon." This professor has just clarified the fish further, and made a new class called "Salmon" that has more specific attributes. Longer nose, reddish flesh, big, lives in the ocean or fresh water, tasty? Probably a salmon.

Finally, a cook comes along and tells the Ph.D., "No, you see this Salmon right here, I'll call her Mary, and I'm going to make a tasty fillet out of her with a nice sauce." Now you have this *instance* of a salmon (which also is an instance of a fish) named Mary turned into something real that is filling your belly. It has become an object.

There you have it: Mary is a kind of salmon that is a kind of fish—object is a class is a class.

How This Looks in Code

This is a weird concept, but to be very honest you only have to worry about it when you make new classes and when you use a class. I will show you two tricks to help you figure out whether something is a class or an object.

First, you need to learn two catch phrases: "is-a" and "has-a." You use the phrase is-a when you talk about objects and classes being related to each other by a class relationship. You use has-a when you talk about objects and classes that are related only because they *reference* each other.

Now, go through this piece of code and replace each ##?? comment with a comment that says whether the next line represents an is-a or a has-a relationship and what that relationship is. In the beginning of the code, I've laid out a few examples, so you just have to write the remaining ones.

Remember, is-a is the relationship between fish and salmon, while has-a is the relationship between salmon and gills.

ex42.py

```
1    ## Animal is-a object (yes, sort of confusing) look at the extra credit
2    class Animal(object):
3        pass
4
5    ## ??
6    class Dog(Animal):
7
8        def __init__(self, name):
9            ## ??
10           self.name = name
11
12   ## ??
13   class Cat(Animal):
14
15       def __init__(self, name):
16           ## ??
17           self.name = name
18
19   ## ??
20   class Person(object):
21
22       def __init__(self, name):
23           ## ??
24           self.name = name
25
```

```
26                  ## Person has-a pet of some kind
27                  self.pet = None
28
29      ## ??
30      class Employee(Person):
31
32          def __init__(self, name, salary):
33              ## ?? hmm what is this strange magic?
34              super(Employee, self).__init__(name)
35              ## ??
36              self.salary = salary
37
38      ## ??
39      class Fish(object):
40          pass
41
42      ## ??
43      class Salmon(Fish):
44          pass
45
46      ## ??
47      class Halibut(Fish):
48          pass
49
50
51      ## rover is-a Dog
52      rover = Dog("Rover")
53
54      ## ??
55      satan = Cat("Satan")
56
57      ## ??
58      mary = Person("Mary")
59
60      ## ??
61      mary.pet = satan
62
63      ## ??
64      frank = Employee("Frank", 120000)
65
66      ## ??
67      frank.pet = rover
68
69      ## ??
70      flipper = Fish()
71
72      ## ??
73      crouse = Salmon()
74
75      ## ??
76      harry = Halibut()
```

About `class Name(object)`

In Python 3, you do not need to add the `(object)` after the name of the class, but the Python community believes in "explicit is better than implicit," so I and other Python experts have decided to include it. You may run into code that does not have `(object)` after simple classes, and those classes are perfectly fine and will work with classes you create that do have `(object)`. At this point it is simply extra documentation and has no impact on how your classes work.

In Python 2, there was a difference between the two types of classes, but now you don't have to worry about it. The only tricky part to using `(object)` involves the mental gymnastics of saying "class Name is a class of type object." That may sound confusing to you now, since it's a class that's a name object that's a class, but don't feel bad about that. Just think of `class Name(object)` as saying "this is a basic simple class," and you'll be fine.

Finally, in the future the styles and tastes of Python programmers may change and this explicit use of `(object)` might be seen as a sign that you are a bad programmer. If that happens, simply stop using it, or tell them, "Python Zen says explicit is better than implicit."

Study Drills

1. Research why Python added this strange object class and what that means.

2. Is it possible to use a class like it's an object?

3. Fill out the animals, fish, and people in this exercise with functions that make them do things. See what happens when functions are in a "base class" like `Animal` versus in, say, `Dog`.

4. Find other people's code and work out all the is-a and has-a relationships.

5. Make some new relationships that are lists and dictionaries so you can also have "has-many" relationships.

6. Do you think there's such thing as an "is-many" relationship? Read about "multiple inheritance," then avoid it if you can.

Common Student Questions

What are these ## ?? comments for?   Those are "fill-in-the-blank" comments that you are supposed to fill in with the right is-a and has-a concepts. Read this exercise again and look at the other comments to see what I mean.

What is the point of `self.pet = None`? That makes sure that the `self.pet` attribute of that class is set to a default of None.

What does `super(Employee, self).__init__(name)` **do?** That's how you can run the `__init__` method of a parent class reliably. Search for "python3.6 super" and read the various advice on it being evil and good for you.

Basic Object-Oriented Analysis and Design

I'm going to describe a process to use when you want to build something using Python, specifically with object-oriented programming (OOP). What I mean by a "process" is that I'll give you a set of steps that you do in order but that you aren't meant to be a slave to and that might not always work for every problem. They are just a good starting point for many programming problems and shouldn't be considered the *only* way to solve these types of problems. This process is just one way to do it that you can follow.

The process is as follows:

1. Write or draw about the problem.
2. Extract key concepts from 1 and research them.
3. Create a class hierarchy and object map for the concepts.
4. Code the classes and a test to run them.
5. Repeat and refine.

The way to look at this process is that it is "top down," meaning it starts from the very abstract loose idea and then slowly refines it until the idea is solid and something you can code.

I start by just writing about the problem and trying to think up anything I can about it. Maybe I'll even draw a diagram or two, maybe a map of some kind, or even write myself a series of emails describing the problem. This gives me a way to express the key concepts in the problem and also explore what I might already know about it.

Then I go through these notes, drawings, and descriptions, and I pull out the key concepts. There's a simple trick to doing this: I make a list of all the *nouns* and *verbs* in my writing and drawings, then write out how they're related. This gives me a good list of names for classes, objects, and functions in the next step. I take this list of concepts and then research any that I don't understand so I can refine them further if needed.

Once I have my list of concepts I create a simple outline/tree of the concepts and how they are related as classes. I can usually take my list of nouns and start asking, "Is this one like other concept nouns? That means they have a common parent class, so what is it called?" I keep doing this until I have a class hierarchy that's just a simple tree list or a diagram. Then I take the *verbs* I have and see if those are function names for each class and put them in my tree.

With this class hierarchy figured out, I sit down and write some basic skeleton code that has just the classes, their functions, and nothing more. I then write a test that runs this code and makes sure the classes I've made make sense and work right. Sometimes I may write the test first, and other times I might write a little test, a little code, a little test, and so on until I have the whole thing built.

Finally, I keep cycling over this process, repeating it and refining as I go, and making it as clear as I can before doing more implementation. If I get stuck at any particular part because of a concept or problem I haven't anticipated, then I sit down and start the process over on just that part to figure it out more before continuing.

I will now go through this process while coming up with a game engine and a game for this exercise.

The Analysis of a Simple Game Engine

The game I want to make is called "Gothons from Planet Percal #25," and it will be a small space adventure game. With nothing more than that concept in my mind, I can explore the idea and figure out how to make the game come to life.

Write or Draw About the Problem

I'm going to write a little paragraph for the game:

"Aliens have invaded a space ship and our hero has to go through a maze of rooms defeating them so he can escape into an escape pod to the planet below. The game will be more like a *Zork* or *Adventure* type game with text outputs and funny ways to die. The game will involve an engine that runs a map full of rooms or scenes. Each room will print its own description when the player enters it and then tell the engine what room to run next out of the map."

At this point I have a good idea for the game and how it would run, so now I want to describe each scene:

Death   This is when the player dies and should be something funny.

Central Corridor   This is the starting point and has a Gothon already standing there that the players have to defeat with a joke before continuing.

Laser Weapon Armory   This is where the hero gets a neutron bomb to blow up the ship before getting to the escape pod. It has a keypad the hero has to guess the number for.

The Bridge   This is another battle scene with a Gothon where the hero places the bomb.

Escape Pod   This is where the hero escapes but only after guessing the right escape pod.

At this point I might draw out a map of these, maybe write more descriptions of each room—whatever comes to mind as I explore the problem.

Extract Key Concepts and Research Them

I now have enough information to extract some of the nouns and analyze their class hierarchy. First I make a list of all the nouns:

- Alien
- Player
- Ship
- Maze
- Room
- Scene
- Gothon
- Escape Pod
- Planet
- Map
- Engine
- Death
- Central Corridor
- Laser Weapon Armory
- The Bridge

I would also possibly go through all the verbs and see if any of them might be good function names, but I'll skip that for now.

At this point I might also research each of these concepts and anything I don't know right now. For example, I might play a few of these types of games and make sure I know how they work. I might research how ships are designed or how bombs work. Maybe I'll research some technical issue like how to store the game's state in a database. After I've done this research I might start over at step 1 based on new information I have and rewrite my description and extract new concepts.

Create a Class Hierarchy and Object Map for the Concepts

Once I have that I turn it into a class hierarchy by asking, "What is similar to other things?" I also ask, "What is basically just another word for another thing?"

Right away I see that "Room" and "Scene" are basically the same thing depending on how I want to do things. I'm going to pick "Scene" for this game. Then I see that all the specific rooms, like "Central Corridor," are basically just Scenes. I see also that Death is basically a Scene, which confirms my choice of "Scene" over "Room," since you can have a death scene, but a death room is kind of odd. "Maze" and "Map" are basically the same, so I'm going to go with "Map" since I used it more often. I don't want to do a battle system, so I'm going to ignore "Alien" and "Player" and save that for later. The "Planet" could also just be another scene instead of something specific.

After all of that thought process I start to make a class hierarchy that looks like this in my text editor:

```
* Map
* Engine
* Scene
    * Death
    * Central Corridor
    * Laser Weapon Armory
    * The Bridge
    * Escape Pod
```

I then go through and figure out what actions are needed on each thing based on verbs in the description. For example, I know from the description I'm going to need a way to "run" the engine, "get the next scene" from the map, get the "opening scene," and "enter" a scene. I'll add those like this:

```
* Map
    - next_scene
    - opening_scene
* Engine
    - play
* Scene
    - enter
    * Death
    * Central Corridor
    * Laser Weapon Armory
    * The Bridge
    * Escape Pod
```

Notice how I just put -enter under Scene since I know that all the scenes under it will inherit it and have to override it later.

Code the Classes and a Test to Run Them

Once I have this tree of classes and some of the functions I open up a source file in my editor and try to write the code for it. Usually I'll just copy-paste the tree into the source file and then edit it into classes. Here's a small example of how this might look at first, with a simple little test at the end of the file.

ex43_classes.py

```
1    class Scene(object):
2
3        def enter(self):
4            pass
```

```
 5
 6
 7    class Engine(object):
 8
 9        def __init__(self, scene_map):
10            pass
11
12        def play(self):
13            pass
14
15    class Death(Scene):
16
17        def enter(self):
18            pass
19
20    class CentralCorridor(Scene):
21
22        def enter(self):
23            pass
24
25    class LaserWeaponArmory(Scene):
26
27        def enter(self):
28            pass
29
30    class TheBridge(Scene):
31
32        def enter(self):
33            pass
34
35    class EscapePod(Scene):
36
37        def enter(self):
38            pass
39
40
41    class Map(object):
42
43        def __init__(self, start_scene):
44            pass
45
46        def next_scene(self, scene_name):
47            pass
48
49        def opening_scene(self):
50            pass
51
52
53    a_map = Map('central_corridor')
54    a_game = Engine(a_map)
55    a_game.play()
```

In this file you can see that I simply replicated the hierarchy I wanted and then added a little bit of code at the end to run it and see if it all works in this basic structure. In the later sections of this exercise you'll fill in the rest of this code and make it work to match the description of the game.

Repeat and Refine

The last step in my little process isn't so much a step as it is a `while-loop`. You don't ever do this as a one-pass operation. Instead you go back over the whole process again and refine it based on information you've learned from later steps. Sometimes I'll get to step 3 and realize that I need to work on 1 and 2 more, so I'll stop and go back and work on those. Sometimes I'll get a flash of inspiration and jump to the end to code up the solution in my head while I have it there, but then I'll go back and do the previous steps to make sure I cover all the possibilities I have.

The other idea in this process is that it's not just something you do at one single level but something that you can do at every level when you run into a particular problem. Let's say I don't know how to write the `Engine.play` method yet. I can stop and do this whole process on *just* that one function to figure out how to write it.

Top Down versus Bottom Up

The process is typically labeled "top down" since it starts at the most abstract concepts (the top) and works its way down to actual implementation. I want you to use this process I just described when analyzing problems in the book from now on, but you should know that there's another way to solve problems in programming that starts with code and goes "up" to the abstract concepts. This other way is labeled "bottom up." Here are the general steps you follow to do this:

1. Take a small piece of the problem; hack on some code and get it to run barely.
2. Refine the code into something more formal with classes and automated tests.
3. Extract the key concepts you're using and research them.
4. Write a description of what's really going on.
5. Go back and refine the code, possibly throwing it out and starting over.
6. Repeat, moving on to some other piece of the problem.

I find this process is better once you're more solid at programming and are naturally thinking in code about problems. This process is very good when you know small pieces of the overall puzzle, but maybe don't have enough information yet about the overall concept. Breaking it down in little pieces and exploring with code then helps you slowly grind away at the problem until you've solved it. However, remember that your solution will probably be meandering and weird, so that's why my version of this process involves going back and finding research, then cleaning things up based on what you've learned.

The Code for "Gothons from Planet Percal #25"

Stop! I'm going to show you my final solution to the preceding problem, but I don't want you to just jump in and type this up. I want *you* to take the rough skeleton code I did and try to make it work based on the description. Once you have your solution then you can come back and see how I did it.

I'm going to break this final file, ex43.py, down into sections and explain each one rather than dump all the code at once.

ex43.py

```
1    from sys import exit
2    from random import randint
3    from textwrap import dedent
```

This is just our basic imports for the game. The only new thing is the import of the dedent function from the textwrap module. This little function will help us write our room descriptions using " " " (triple-quote) strings. It simply strips leading white-space from the beginnings of lines in a string. Without this function, using " " " style strings fails because they are indented on the *screen* the same level as in the *Python* code.

ex43.py

```
1    class Scene(object):
2
3        def enter(self):
4            print("This scene is not yet configured.")
5            print("Subclass it and implement enter().")
6            exit(1)
```

As you saw in the skeleton code, I have a base class for Scene that will have the common things that all scenes do. In this simple program they don't do much, so this is more a demonstration of what you would do to make a base class.

ex43.py

```
1    class Engine(object):
2
3        def __init__(self, scene_map):
4            self.scene_map = scene_map
5
6        def play(self):
7            current_scene = self.scene_map.opening_scene()
8            last_scene = self.scene_map.next_scene('finished')
9
10           while current_scene != last_scene:
11               next_scene_name = current_scene.enter()
12               current_scene = self.scene_map.next_scene(next_scene_name)
13
14           # be sure to print out the last scene
15           current_scene.enter()
```

I also have my Engine class, and you can see how I'm already using the methods for Map.opening_scene and Map.next_scene. Because I've done a bit of planning I can just assume I'll write those and then use them before I've written the Map class.

ex43.py

```
1    class Death(Scene):
2
3        quips = [
4            "You died.  You kinda suck at this.",
5            "Your Mom would be proud...if she were smarter.",
6            "Such a luser.",
7            "I have a small puppy that's better at this.",
8            "You're worse than your Dad's jokes."
9
10       ]
11
12       def enter(self):
13           print(Death.quips[randint(0, len(self.quips)-1)])
14           exit(1)
```

My first scene is the odd scene named Death, which shows you the simplest kind of scene you can write.

ex43.py

```
1    class CentralCorridor(Scene):
2
3        def enter(self):
4            print(dedent("""
5                The Gothons of Planet Percal #25 have invaded your ship and
6                destroyed your entire crew.  You are the last surviving
7                member and your last mission is to get the neutron destruct
8                bomb from the Weapons Armory, put it in the bridge, and
9                blow the ship up after getting into an escape pod.
10
11               You're running down the central corridor to the Weapons
12               Armory when a Gothon jumps out, red scaly skin, dark grimy
13               teeth, and evil clown costume flowing around his hate
14               filled body.  He's blocking the door to the Armory and
15               about to pull a weapon to blast you.
16               """))
17
18           action = input("> ")
19
20           if action == "shoot!":
21               print(dedent("""
22                   Quick on the draw you yank out your blaster and fire
23                   it at the Gothon.  His clown costume is flowing and
24                   moving around his body, which throws off your aim.
25                   Your laser hits his costume but misses him entirely.
26                   This completely ruins his brand new costume his mother
```

```
27                    bought him, which makes him fly into an insane rage
28                    and blast you repeatedly in the face until you are
29                    dead.  Then he eats you.
30                    """))
31              return 'death'
32
33          elif action == "dodge!":
34              print(dedent("""
35                    Like a world class boxer you dodge, weave, slip and
36                    slide right as the Gothon's blaster cranks a laser
37                    past your head.  In the middle of your artful dodge
38                    your foot slips and you bang your head on the metal
39                    wall and pass out.  You wake up shortly after only to
40                    die as the Gothon stomps on your head and eats you.
41                    """))
42              return 'death'
43
44          elif action == "tell a joke":
45              print(dedent("""
46                    Lucky for you they made you learn Gothon insults in
47                    the academy.  You tell the one Gothon joke you know:
48                    Lbhe zbgure vf fb sng, jura fur fvgf nebhaq gur ubhfr,
49                    fur fvgf nebhaq gur ubhfr.  The Gothon stops, tries
50                    not to laugh, then busts out laughing and can't move.
51                    While he's laughing you run up and shoot him square in
52                    the head putting him down, then jump through the
53                    Weapon Armory door.
54                    """))
55              return 'laser_weapon_armory'
56
57          else:
58              print("DOES NOT COMPUTE!")
59              return 'central_corridor'
```

After that I've created the `CentralCorridor`, which is the start of the game. I'm doing the scenes for the game before the Map because I need to reference them later. You should also see how I use the `dedent` function on line 4. Try removing it later to see what it does.

ex43.py

```
1    class LaserWeaponArmory(Scene):
2
3        def enter(self):
4            print(dedent("""
5                    You do a dive roll into the Weapon Armory, crouch and scan
6                    the room for more Gothons that might be hiding.  It's dead
7                    quiet, too quiet.  You stand up and run to the far side of
8                    the room and find the neutron bomb in its container.
9                    There's a keypad lock on the box and you need the code to
10                   get the bomb out.  If you get the code wrong 10 times then
11                   the lock closes forever and you can't get the bomb.  The
```

```
12                       code is 3 digits.
13                       """))
14
15              code = f"{randint(1,9)}{randint(1,9)}{randint(1,9)}"
16              guess = input("[keypad]> ")
17              guesses = 0
18
19              while guess != code and guesses < 10:
20                  print("BZZZZEDDD!")
21                  guesses += 1
22                  guess = input("[keypad]> ")
23
24              if guess == code:
25                  print(dedent("""
26                      The container clicks open and the seal breaks, letting
27                      gas out.  You grab the neutron bomb and run as fast as
28                      you can to the bridge where you must place it in the
29                      right spot.
30                      """))
31                  return 'the_bridge'
32              else:
33                  print(dedent("""
34                      The lock buzzes one last time and then you hear a
35                      sickening melting sound as the mechanism is fused
36                      together.  You decide to sit there, and finally the
37                      Gothons blow up the ship from their ship and you die.
38                      """))
39                  return 'death'
40
41
42
43      class TheBridge(Scene):
44
45          def enter(self):
46              print(dedent("""
47                  You burst onto the Bridge with the netron destruct bomb
48                  under your arm and surprise 5 Gothons who are trying to
49                  take control of the ship.  Each of them has an even uglier
50                  clown costume than the last.  They haven't pulled their
51                  weapons out yet, as they see the active bomb under your
52                  arm and don't want to set it off.
53                  """))
54
55              action = input("> ")
56
57              if action == "throw the bomb":
58                  print(dedent("""
59                      In a panic you throw the bomb at the group of Gothons
60                      and make a leap for the door.  Right as you drop it a
61                      Gothon shoots you right in the back killing you.  As
```

```
62              you die you see another Gothon frantically try to
63              disarm the bomb. You die knowing they will probably
64              blow up when it goes off.
65              """))
66          return 'death'
67
68      elif action == "slowly place the bomb":
69          print(dedent("""
70              You point your blaster at the bomb under your arm and
71              the Gothons put their hands up and start to sweat.
72              You inch backward to the door, open it, and then
73              carefully place the bomb on the floor, pointing your
74              blaster at it.  You then jump back through the door,
75              punch the close button and blast the lock so the
76              Gothons can't get out.  Now that the bomb is placed
77              you run to the escape pod to get off this tin can.
78              """))
79
80          return 'escape_pod'
81      else:
82          print("DOES NOT COMPUTE!")
83          return "the_bridge"
84
85
86  class EscapePod(Scene):
87
88      def enter(self):
89          print(dedent("""
90              You rush through the ship desperately trying to make it to
91              the escape pod before the whole ship explodes.  It seems
92              like hardly any Gothons are on the ship, so your run is
93              clear of interference.  You get to the chamber with the
94              escape pods, and now need to pick one to take.  Some of
95              them could be damaged but you don't have time to look.
96              There's 5 pods, which one do you take?
97              """))
98
99          good_pod = randint(1,5)
100         guess = input("[pod #]> ")
101
102
103         if int(guess) != good_pod:
104             print(dedent("""
105                 You jump into pod {guess} and hit the eject button.
106                 The pod escapes out into the void of space, then
107                 implodes as the hull ruptures, crushing your body into
108                 jam jelly.
109                 """))
110             return 'death'
111         else:
```

```
112             print(dedent("""
113                 You jump into pod {guess} and hit the eject button.
114                 The pod easily slides out into space heading to the
115                 planet below.  As it flies to the planet, you look
116                 back and see your ship implode then explode like a
117                 bright star, taking out the Gothon ship at the same
118                 time.  You won!
119                 """))
120
121             return 'finished'
122
123     class Finished(Scene):
124
125         def enter(self):
126             print("You won! Good job.")
127             return 'finished'
```

This is the rest of the game's scenes, and since I know I need them and have thought about how they'll flow together I'm able to code them up directly.

Incidentally, I wouldn't just type all this code in. Remember I said to try and build this incrementally, one little bit at a time. I'm just showing you the final result.

ex43.py

```
1     class Map(object):
2
3         scenes = {
4             'central_corridor': CentralCorridor(),
5             'laser_weapon_armory': LaserWeaponArmory(),
6             'the_bridge': TheBridge(),
7             'escape_pod': EscapePod(),
8             'death': Death(),
9             'finished': Finished(),
10        }
11
12        def __init__(self, start_scene):
13            self.start_scene = start_scene
14
15        def next_scene(self, scene_name):
16            val = Map.scenes.get(scene_name)
17            return val
18
19        def opening_scene(self):
20            return self.next_scene(self.start_scene)
```

After that I have my Map class, and you can see it is storing each scene by name in a dictionary, and then I refer to that dict with `Map.scenes`. This is also why the map comes after the scenes because the dictionary has to refer to the scenes, so they have to exist.

```
1    a_map = Map('central_corridor')
2    a_game = Engine(a_map)
3    a_game.play()
```

Finally I've got my code that runs the game by making a Map, then handing that map to an Engine before calling play to make the game work.

What You Should See

Make sure you understand the game and that you tried to solve it yourself first. One thing to do if you're stumped is cheat a little by reading my code, then continue trying to solve it yourself.

When I run my game it looks like this:

```
$ python3.6 ex43.py

The Gothons of Planet Percal #25 have invaded your ship and
destroyed your entire crew.  You are the last surviving
member and your last mission is to get the neutron destruct
bomb from the Weapons Armory, put it in the bridge, and
blow the ship up after getting into an escape pod.

You're running down the central corridor to the Weapons
Armory when a Gothon jumps out, red scaly skin, dark grimy
teeth, and evil clown costume flowing around his hate
filled body.  He's blocking the door to the Armory and
about to pull a weapon to blast you.

>  dodge!

Like a world class boxer you dodge, weave, slip and
slide right as the Gothon's blaster cranks a laser
past your head.  In the middle of your artful dodge
your foot slips and you bang your head on the metal
wall and pass out.  You wake up shortly after only to
die as the Gothon stomps on your head and eats you.

You're worse than your Dad's jokes.
```

Study Drills

1. Change it! Maybe you hate this game. It could be too violent, or maybe you aren't into sci-fi. Get the game working, then change it to what you like. This is your computer; you make it do what you want.

2. I have a bug in this code. Why is the door lock guessing 11 times?

3. Explain how returning the next room works.

4. Add cheat codes to the game so you can get past the more difficult rooms. I can do this with two words on one line.

5. Go back to my description and analysis, then try to build a small combat system for the hero and the various Gothons he encounters.

6. This is actually a small version of something called a "finite state machine." Read about them. They might not make sense, but try anyway.

Common Student Questions

Where can I find stories for my own games?   You can make them up, just like you would tell a story to a friend. Or you can take simple scenes from a book or movie you like.

Inheritance versus Composition

In the fairy tales about heroes defeating evil villains there's always a dark forest of some kind. It could be a cave, a forest, another planet, just some place that everyone knows the hero shouldn't go. Of course, shortly after the villain is introduced you find out, yes, the hero has to go to that stupid forest to kill the bad guy. It seems the hero just keeps getting into situations that require him to risk his life in this evil forest.

You rarely read fairy tales about the heroes who are smart enough to just avoid the whole situation entirely. You never hear a hero say, "Wait a minute, if I leave to make my fortunes on the high seas, leaving Buttercup behind, I could die and then she'd have to marry some ugly prince named Humperdink. Humperdink! I think I'll stay here and start a Farm Boy for Rent business." If he did that there'd be no fire swamp, dying, reanimation, sword fights, giants, or any kind of story really. Because of this, the forest in these stories seems to exist like a black hole that drags the hero in no matter what they do.

In object-oriented programming, inheritance is the evil forest. Experienced programmers know to avoid this evil because they know that deep inside the Dark Forest Inheritance is the Evil Queen Multiple Inheritance. She likes to eat software and programmers with her massive complexity teeth, chewing on the flesh of the fallen. But the forest is so powerful and so tempting that nearly every programmer has to go into it and try to make it out alive with the Evil Queen's head before they can call themselves real programmers. You just can't resist the Inheritance Forest's pull, so you go in. After the adventure you learn to just stay out of that stupid forest and bring an army if you are ever forced to go in again.

This is basically a funny way to say that I'm going to teach you something you should use carefully called *inheritance*. Programmers who are currently in the forest battling the Queen will probably tell you that you have to go in. They say this because they need your help since what they've created is probably too much for them to handle. But you should always remember this:

> Most of the uses of inheritance can be simplified or replaced with composition, and multiple inheritance should be avoided at all costs.

What Is Inheritance?

Inheritance is used to indicate that one class will get most or all of its features from a parent class. This happens implicitly whenever you write `class Foo(Bar)`, which says "Make a class Foo that inherits from Bar." When you do this, the language makes any action that you do on instances of Foo also work as if they were done to an instance of Bar. Doing this lets you put common functionality in the Bar class, then specialize that functionality in the Foo class as needed.

When you are doing this kind of specialization, there are three ways that the parent and child classes can interact:

1. Actions on the child imply an action on the parent.

2. Actions on the child override the action on the parent.

3. Actions on the child alter the action on the parent.

I will now demonstrate each of these in order and show you code for them.

Implicit Inheritance

First I will show you the implicit actions that happen when you define a function in the parent but *not* in the child.

ex44a.py

```
1    class Parent(object):
2
3        def implicit(self):
4            print("PARENT implicit()")
5
6    class Child(Parent):
7        pass
8
9    dad = Parent()
10   son = Child()
11
12   dad.implicit()
13   son.implicit()
```

The use of pass under the class Child: is how you tell Python that you want an empty block. This creates a class named Child but says that there's nothing new to define in it. Instead it will inherit all of its behavior from Parent. When you run this code you get the following:

Exercise 44a Session

```
$ python3.6 ex44a.py
PARENT implicit()
PARENT implicit()
```

Notice how even though I'm calling son.implicit() on line 13 and even though Child does *not* have an implicit function defined, it still works, and it calls the one defined in Parent. This shows you that if you put functions in a base class (i.e., Parent), then all subclasses (i.e., Child) will automatically get those features. Very handy for repetitive code you need in many classes.

Override Explicitly

The problem with having functions called implicitly is sometimes you want the child to behave differently. In this case you want to override the function in the child, effectively replacing the functionality. To do this just define a function with the same name in `Child`. Here's an example:

ex44b.py

```
 1    class Parent(object):
 2
 3        def override(self):
 4            print("PARENT override()")
 5
 6    class Child(Parent):
 7
 8        def override(self):
 9            print("CHILD override()")
10
11    dad = Parent()
12    son = Child()
13
14    dad.override()
15    son.override()
```

In this example I have a function named `override` in both classes, so let's see what happens when I run it.

Exercise 44b Session

```
$ python3.6 ex44b.py
PARENT override()
CHILD override()
```

As you can see, when line 14 runs, it runs the `Parent.override` function because that variable (dad) is a `Parent`. But when line 15 runs, it prints out the `Child.override` messages because `son` is an instance of `Child` and `Child` overrides that function by defining its own version.

Take a break right now and try playing with these two concepts before continuing.

Alter Before or After

The third way to use inheritance is a special case of overriding where you want to alter the behavior before or after the `Parent` class's version runs. You first override the function just like in the last example, but then you use a Python built-in function named `super` to get the `Parent` version to call. Here's the example of doing that so you can make sense of this description:

ex44c.py

```
1   class Parent(object):
2
3       def altered(self):
4           print("PARENT altered()")
5
6   class Child(Parent):
7
8       def altered(self):
9           print("CHILD, BEFORE PARENT altered()")
10          super(Child, self).altered()
11          print("CHILD, AFTER PARENT altered()")
12
13  dad = Parent()
14  son = Child()
15
16  dad.altered()
17  son.altered()
```

The important lines here are 9–11, where in the Child I do the following when son.altered() is called:

1. Because I've overridden Parent.altered the Child.altered version runs, and line 9 executes like you'd expect.

2. In this case I want to do a before and after, so after line 9 I want to use super to get the Parent.altered version.

3. On line 10 I call super(Child, self).altered(), which is aware of inheritance and will get the Parent class for you. You should be able to read this as "call super with arguments Child and self, then call the function altered on whatever it returns."

4. At this point, the Parent.altered version of the function runs, and that prints out the Parent message.

5. Finally, this returns from the Parent.altered, and the Child.altered function continues to print out the after message.

If you run this, you should see this:

Exercise 44c Session

```
$ python3.6 ex44c.py
PARENT altered()
CHILD, BEFORE PARENT altered()
PARENT altered()
CHILD, AFTER PARENT altered()
```

All Three Combined

To demonstrate all of these, I have a final version that shows each kind of interaction from inheritance in one file:

ex44d.py

```
 1  class Parent(object):
 2
 3      def override(self):
 4          print("PARENT override()")
 5
 6      def implicit(self):
 7          print("PARENT implicit()")
 8
 9      def altered(self):
10          print("PARENT altered()")
11
12  class Child(Parent):
13
14      def override(self):
15          print("CHILD override()")
16
17      def altered(self):
18          print("CHILD, BEFORE PARENT altered()")
19          super(Child, self).altered()
20          print("CHILD, AFTER PARENT altered()")
21
22  dad = Parent()
23  son = Child()
24
25  dad.implicit()
26  son.implicit()
27
28  dad.override()
29  son.override()
30
31  dad.altered()
32  son.altered()
```

Go through each line of this code, and write a comment explaining what that line does and whether it's an override or not. Then run it and confirm you get what you expected:

Exercise 44d Session

```
$ python3.6 ex44d.py
PARENT implicit()
PARENT implicit()
PARENT override()
CHILD override()
```

```
PARENT altered()
CHILD, BEFORE PARENT altered()
PARENT altered()
CHILD, AFTER PARENT altered()
```

The Reason for `super()`

This should seem like common sense, but then we get into trouble with a thing called multiple inheritance. Multiple inheritance is when you define a class that inherits from one or *more* classes, like this:

```
class SuperFun(Child, BadStuff):
    pass
```

This is like saying, "Make a class named `SuperFun` that inherits from the classes `Child` and `BadStuff` at the same time."

In this case, whenever you have implicit actions on any `SuperFun` instance, Python has to look up the possible function in the class hierarchy for both `Child` and `BadStuff`, but it needs to do this in a consistent order. To do this Python uses "method resolution order" (MRO) and an algorithm called C3 to get it straight.

Because the MRO is complex and a well-defined algorithm is used, Python can't leave it to you to get the MRO right. Instead, Python gives you the `super()` function, which handles all of this for you in the places that you need the altering type of actions as I did in `Child.altered`. With `super()` you don't have to worry about getting this right, and Python will find the right function for you.

Using `super()` with `__init__`

The most common use of `super()` is actually in `__init__` functions in base classes. This is usually the only place where you need to do some things in a child, then complete the initialization in the parent. Here's a quick example of doing that in the `Child`:

```
class Child(Parent):

    def __init__(self, stuff):
        self.stuff = stuff
        super(Child, self).__init__()
```

This is pretty much the same as the `Child.altered` example above, except I'm setting some variables in the `__init__` before having the `Parent` initialize with its `Parent.__init__`.

Composition

Inheritance is useful, but another way to do the exact same thing is just to *use* other classes and modules, rather than rely on implicit inheritance. If you look at the three ways to exploit inheritance, two of the three involve writing new code to replace or alter functionality. This can easily be replicated by just calling functions in a module. Here's an example of doing this:

ex44e.py

```python
 1    class Other(object):
 2
 3        def override(self):
 4            print("OTHER override()")
 5
 6        def implicit(self):
 7            print("OTHER implicit()")
 8
 9        def altered(self):
10            print("OTHER altered()")
11
12    class Child(object):
13
14        def __init__(self):
15            self.other = Other()
16
17        def implicit(self):
18            self.other.implicit()
19
20        def override(self):
21            print("CHILD override()")
22
23        def altered(self):
24            print("CHILD, BEFORE OTHER altered()")
25            self.other.altered()
26            print("CHILD, AFTER OTHER altered()")
27
28    son = Child()
29
30    son.implicit()
31    son.override()
32    son.altered()
```

In this code I'm not using the name `Parent`, since there is *not* a parent-child is-a relationship. This is a has-a relationship, where `Child` has-a `Other` that it uses to get its work done. When I run this I get the following output:

Exercise 44e Session

```
$ python3.6 ex44e.py
OTHER implicit()
CHILD override()
```

```
CHILD, BEFORE OTHER altered()
OTHER altered()
CHILD, AFTER OTHER altered()
```

You can see that most of the code in `Child` and `Other` is the same to accomplish the same thing. The only difference is that I had to define a `Child.implicit` function to do that one action. I could then ask myself if I need this `Other` to be a class, and could I just make it into a module named `other.py`?

When to Use Inheritance or Composition

The question of "inheritance versus composition" comes down to an attempt to solve the problem of reusable code. You don't want to have duplicated code all over your software, since that's not clean and efficient. Inheritance solves this problem by creating a mechanism for you to have implied features in base classes. Composition solves this by giving you modules and the capability to call functions in other classes.

If both solutions solve the problem of reuse, then which one is appropriate in which situations? The answer is incredibly subjective, but I'll give you my three guidelines for when to do which:

1. Avoid multiple inheritance at all costs, as it's too complex to be reliable. If you're stuck with it, then be prepared to know the class hierarchy and spend time finding where everything is coming from.

2. Use composition to package code into modules that are used in many different unrelated places and situations.

3. Use inheritance only when there are clearly related reusable pieces of code that fit under a single common concept or if you have to because of something you're using.

Do not be a slave to these rules. The thing to remember about object-oriented programming is that it is entirely a social convention programmers have created to package and share code. Because it's a social convention, but one that's codified in Python, you may be forced to avoid these rules because of the people you work with. In that case, find out how they use things and then just adapt to the situation.

Study Drills

There is only one Study Drill for this exercise because it is a big exercise. Go and read http://www .python.org/dev/peps/pep-0008/ and start trying to use it in your code. You'll notice that some of it is different from what you've been learning in this book, but now you should be able to understand their recommendations and use them in your own code. The rest of the code in this book may or may not follow these guidelines depending on whether it makes the code more confusing. I suggest you also do this, as comprehension is more important than impressing everyone with your knowledge of esoteric style rules.

Common Student Questions

How do I get better at solving problems that I haven't seen before?   The only way to get better at solving problems is to solve as many problems as you can *by yourself*. Typically people hit a difficult problem and then rush out to find an answer. This is fine when you have to get things done, but if you have the time to solve it yourself, then take that time. Stop and bang your head against the problem for as long as possible, trying every possible thing, until you solve it or give up. After that the answers you find will be more satisfying, and you'll eventually get better at solving problems.

Aren't objects just copies of classes?   In some languages (like JavaScript) that is true. These are called prototype languages, and there are not many differences between objects and classes other than usage. In Python, however, classes act as templates that "mint" new objects, similar to how coins are minted using a die (template).

You Make a Game

Y ou need to start learning to feed yourself. Hopefully as you have worked through this book, you have learned that all the information you need is on the internet. You just have to go search for it. The only thing you have been missing are the right words and what to look for when you search. Now you should have a sense of it, so it's about time you struggled through a big project and tried to get it working.

Here are your requirements:

1. Make a different game from the one I made.

2. Use more than one file, and use `import` to use them. Make sure you know what that is.

3. Use *one class per room* and give the classes names that fit their purposes (like `GoldRoom`, `KoiPondRoom`).

4. Your runner will need to know about these rooms, so make a class that runs them and knows about them. There're plenty of ways to do this, but consider having each room return what room is next or setting a variable of what room is next.

Other than that I leave it to you. Spend a whole week on this and make it the best game you can. Use classes, functions, dicts, lists, anything you can to make it nice. The purpose of this lesson is to teach you how to structure classes that need other classes inside other files.

Remember, I'm not telling you *exactly* how to do this because you have to do this yourself. Go figure it out. Programming is problem solving, and that means trying things, experimenting, failing, scrapping your work, and trying again. When you get stuck, ask for help and show people your code. If they are mean to you, ignore them, and focus on the people who are not mean and offer to help. Keep working it and cleaning it until it's good, then show it some more.

Good luck, and see you in a week with your game.

Evaluating Your Game

In this exercise you will evaluate the game you just made. Maybe you got partway through it and you got stuck. Maybe you got it working but just barely. Either way, we're going to go through a bunch of things you should know now and make sure you covered them in your game. We're going to study properly formatting a class, common conventions in using classes, and a lot of "textbook" knowledge.

Why would I have you try to do it yourself and then show you how to do it right? From now on in the book I'm going to try to make you self-sufficient. I've been holding your hand mostly this whole time, and

I can't do that for much longer. I'm now instead going to give you things to do, have you do them on your own, and then give you ways to improve what you did.

You will struggle at first and probably be very frustrated, but stick with it and eventually you will build a mind for solving problems. You will start to find creative solutions to problems rather than just copy solutions out of textbooks.

Function Style

All the other rules I've taught you about how to make a nice function apply here, but add these things:

- For various reasons, programmers call functions that are part of classes "methods." It's mostly marketing, but just be warned that every time you say "function" they'll annoyingly correct you and say "method." If they get too annoying, just ask them to demonstrate the mathematical basis that determines how a "method" is different from a "function" and they'll shut up.

- When you work with classes much of your time is spent talking about making the class "do things." Instead of naming a function after what the function does, instead name it as if it's a command you are giving to the class. For example, pop is saying "Hey list, pop this off." It isn't called `remove_from_end_of_list` because even though that's what it does, that's not a *command* to a list.

- Keep your functions small and simple. For some reason when people start learning about classes they forget this.

Class Style

- Your class should use "camel case," as in `SuperGoldFactory`, rather than "underscore format," as in `super_gold_factory`.

- Try not to do too much in your `__init__` functions. It makes them harder to use.

- Your other functions should use underscore format, so write `my_awesome_hair` and not `myawesomehair` or `MyAwesomeHair`.

- Be consistent in how you organize your function arguments. If your class has to deal with users, dogs, and cats, keep that order throughout unless it really doesn't make sense. If you have one function that takes (`dog, cat, user`) and the other takes (`user, cat, dog`), it'll be hard to use.

- Try not to use variables that come from the module or globals. They should be fairly self-contained.

- A foolish consistency is the hobgoblin of little minds. Consistency is good, but foolishly following some idiotic mantra because everyone else does is bad style. Think for yourself.

- Always, *always* have `class Name(object)` format or else you will be in big trouble.

Code Style

- Give your code vertical space so people can read it. You will find some very bad programmers who are able to write reasonable code but who do not add *any* spaces. This is bad style in any language because the human eye and brain use space and vertical alignment to scan and separate visual elements. Not having space is the same as giving your code an awesome camouflage paint job.

- If you can't read it out loud, it's probably hard to read. If you are having a problem making something easy to use, try reading it out loud. Not only does this force you to slow down and really read it, but it also helps you find difficult passages and things to change for readability.

- Try to do what other people are doing in Python until you find your own style.

- Once you find your own style, do not be a jerk about it. Working with other people's code is part of being a programmer, and other people have really bad taste. Trust me, you will probably have really bad taste, too, and not even realize it.

- If you find someone who writes code in a style you like, try writing something that mimics that style.

Good Comments

- Programmers will tell you that your code should be readable enough that you do not need comments. They'll then tell you in their most official sounding voice, "Ergo one should never write comments or documentation. QED." Those programmers are either consultants who get paid more if other people can't use their code, or incompetents who tend to never work with other people. Ignore them and write comments.

- When you write comments, describe *why* you are doing what you are doing. The code already says how, so why you did things the way you did is more important.

- When you write doc comments for your functions, make the comments documentation for someone who will have to use your code. You do not have to go crazy, but a nice little sentence about what someone can do with that function helps a lot.

- While comments are good, too many are bad, and you have to maintain them. Keep your comments relatively short and to the point, and if you change a function, review the comment to make sure it's still correct.

Evaluate Your Game

I want you to now pretend you are me. Adopt a very stern look, print out your code, and take a red pen and mark every mistake you find, including anything from this exercise and from other guidelines you've read so far. Once you are done marking your code up, I want you to fix everything you came up with. Then repeat this a couple of times, looking for anything that could be better. Use all the tricks I've given you to break your code down into the smallest, tiniest little analysis you can.

The purpose of this exercise is to train your attention to detail on classes. Once you are done with this bit of code, find someone else's code and do the same thing. Go through a printed copy of some part of it and point out all the mistakes and style errors you find. Then fix it and see if your fixes can be done without breaking that program.

I want you to do nothing but evaluate and fix code for the week—your own code and other people's. It'll be pretty hard work, but when you are done your brain will be wired tight like a boxer's hands.

A Project Skeleton

This will be where you start learning how to set up a good project "skeleton" directory. This skeleton directory will have all the basics you need to get a new project up and running. It will have your project layout, automated tests, modules, and install scripts. When you go to make a new project, just copy this directory to a new name and edit the files to get started.

macOS/Linux Setup

Before you can begin this exercise you need to install some software for Python by using a tool called pip3.6 (or just pip) to install new modules. The pip3.6 command should be included with your python3.6 installation. You'll want to verify this using this command:

```
$ pip3.6 list
pip (9.0.1)
setuptools (28.8.0)
$
```

You can ignore any deprecation warning if you see it. You may also see other tools installed, but the base should be pip and setuptools. Once you've verified this you can then install virtualenv:

```
$ sudo pip3.6 install virtualenv
Password:
Collecting virtualenv
  Downloading virtualenv—15.1.0—py2.py3—none—any.whl (1.8MB)
    100% |||||||||||||||||||||||||||||||||| 1.8MB 1.1MB/s
Installing collected packages: virtualenv
Successfully installed virtualenv—15.1.0
$
```

This is for Linux or macOS systems. If you're on Linux/macOS, you'll want to run the following command to make sure you use the correct virtualenv:

```
$ whereis virtualenv
/Library/Frameworks/Python.framework/Versions/3.6/bin/virtualenv
```

You should see something like the above on macOS, but Linux will be variable. On Linux you might have an actual virtualenv3.6 command, or you may be better off installing a package for it from your package management system.

Once you've installed `virtualenv` you can use it to create a "fake" Python installation, which makes it easier to manage versions of your packages for different projects. First, run this command, and I'll explain what it's doing:

```
$ mkdir ~/.venvs
$ virtualenv —system—site—packages ~/.venvs/lpthw
$ . ~/.venvs/lpthw/bin/activate
(lpthw) $
```

Here's what's going on line by line:

1. You create a directory called `.venvs` in your HOME `~/` to store all your virtual environments.
2. You run `virtualenv` and tell it to include the system site packages (`--system-site-packages`), then instruct it to build the virtualenv in `~/.venvs/lpthw`.
3. You then "source" the `lpthw` virtual environment by using the `.` operator in `bash`, followed by the `~/.venvs/lpthw/bin/activate` script.
4. Finally, your prompt changes to include (`lpthw`), so you know that you're using that virtual environment.

Now you can see where things are installed:

```
(lpthw) $ which python
/Users/zedshaw/.venvs/lpthw/bin/python
(lpthw) $ python
Python 3.6.0rc2 (v3.6.0rc2:800a67f7806d, Dec 16 2016, 14:12:21)
[GCC 4.2.1 (Apple Inc. build 5666) (dot 3)] on darwin
Type "help", "copyright", "credits" or "license" for more information.
>>> quit()
(lpthw) $
```

You can see that the `python` that gets run is installed in the `/Users/zedshaw/.venvs/lpthw/bin/python` directory instead of the original location. This also solves the problem of having to type `python3.6` since it installs both:

```
$ which python3.6
/Users/zedshaw/.venvs/lpthw/bin/python3.6
(lpthw) $
```

You'll find the same thing for `virtualenv` and `pip` commands. The final step in this setup is to install `nose`, a testing framework we'll use in this exercise:

```
$ pip install nose
Collecting nose
```

```
  Downloading nose—1.3.7—py3—none—any.whl (154kB)
    100% ||||||||||||||||||||||||||||||||| 163kB 3.2MB/s
Installing collected packages: nose
Successfully installed nose—1.3.7
(lpthw) $
```

Windows 10 Setup

The Windows 10 install is a little simpler than on Linux or macOS, but only if you have *one* version of
Python installed. If you have both Python 3.6 and Python 2.7 installed then you are on your own as it
is much too difficult to manage multiple installations. If you have followed the book so far and have only
Python 3.6, then here's what you do. First, change to your home directory and confirm you're running
the right version of `python`:

```
> cd ~
> python
Python 3.6.0 (v3.6.0:41df79263a11, Dec 23 2016, 08:06:12)
    [MSC v.1900 64 bit (AMD64)] on win32
Type "help", "copyright", "credits" or "license" for more information.
>>> quit()
```

Then you'll want to run `pip` to confirm you have a basic install:

```
> pip list
pip (9.0.1)
setuptools (28.8.0)
```

You can safely ignore any deprecation warning, and it's alright if you have other packages installed. Next,
you'll install `virtualenv` for setting up simple virtual environments for the rest of the book:

```
> pip install virtualenv
Collecting virtualenv
  Using cached virtualenv—15.1.0—py2.py3—none—any.whl
Installing collected packages: virtualenv
Successfully installed virtualenv—15.1.0
```

Once you have `virtualenv` installed you'll need to make a `.venvs` directory and fill it with a virtual
environment:

```
> mkdir .venvs
> virtualenv —system—site—packages .venvs/lpthw
Using base prefix
    'c:\\users\\zedsh\\appdata\\local\\programs\\python\\python36'
New python executable in
    C:\Users\zedshaw\.venvs\lpthw\Scripts\python.exe
Installing setuptools, pip, wheel...done.
```

Those two commands create a .venvs folder for storing different virtual environments and then create your first one named lpthw. A virtual environment (virtualenv) is a "fake" place to install software so that you can have different versions of different packages for each project you're working on. Once you have the virtualenv set up you need to activate it:

```
> .\.venvs\lpthw\Scripts\activate
```

That will run the activate script for PowerShell, which configures the lpthw virtualenv for your current shell. Every time you want to use your software for the book you'll run this command. You'll notice in our next command that there is now a (lpthw) added to the PowerShell prompt showing you which virtualenv you're using. Finally, you just need to install nose for running tests later:

```
(lpthw) > pip install nose
Collecting nose
  Downloading nose-1.3.7-py3-none-any.whl (154kB)
     100% |||||||||||||||||||||||||||||||||||| 163kB 1.2MB/s
Installing collected packages: nose
Successfully installed nose-1.3.7
(lpthw) >
```

You'll see that this installs nose, except pip will install it into your .venvs\lpthw virtual environment instead of the main system packages directory. This lets you install conflicting versions of Python packages for each project you work on without infecting your main system configuration.

Creating the Skeleton Project Directory

First, create the structure of your skeleton directory with these commands:

```
$ mkdir projects
$ cd projects/
$ mkdir skeleton
$ cd skeleton
$ mkdir bin NAME tests docs
```

I use a directory named projects to store all the various things I'm working on. Inside that directory I have my skeleton directory that I put the basis of my projects into. The directory NAME will be renamed to whatever you are calling your project's main module when you use the skeleton.

Next, we need to set up some initial files. Here's how you do that on Linux/macOS:

```
$ touch NAME/__init__.py
$ touch tests/__init__.py
```

Here's the same thing on Windows PowerShell:

```
$ new-item -type file NAME/__init__.py
$ new-item -type file tests/__init__.py
```

That creates an empty Python module directory we can put our code in. Then we need to create a `setup.py` file we can use to install our project later if we want:

setup.py

```
1   try:
2       from setuptools import setup
3   except ImportError:
4       from distutils.core import setup
5
6   config = {
7       'description': 'My Project',
8       'author': 'My Name',
9       'url': 'URL to get it at.',
10      'download_url': 'Where to download it.',
11      'author_email': 'My email.',
12      'version': '0.1',
13      'install_requires': ['nose'],
14      'packages': ['NAME'],
15      'scripts': [],
16      'name': 'projectname'
17  }
18
19  setup(**config)
```

Edit this file so that it has your contact information and is ready to go for when you copy it.

Finally, you will want a simple skeleton file for tests named `tests/NAME_tests.py`:

NAME_tests.py

```
1   from nose.tools import *
2   import NAME
3
4   def setup():
5       print("SETUP!")
6
7   def teardown():
8       print("TEAR DOWN!")
9
10  def test_basic():
11      print("I RAN!")
```

Final Directory Structure

When you are done setting all of this up, your directory should look like mine here:

```
skeleton/
    NAME/
```

```
    __init__.py
bin/
docs/
setup.py
tests/
    NAME_tests.py
    __init__.py
```

And from now on, you should run your commands from this directory. If you can't, do ls -R and if you don't see this same structure, then you are in the wrong place. For example, people commonly go into the tests/ directory to try to run files there, which won't work. To run your application's tests, you would need to be *above* tests/ and this location I have above. So, if you try this:

```
$ cd tests/    # WRONG! WRONG! WRONG!
$ nosetests
```

```
Ran 0 tests in 0.000s

OK
```

That is *wrong*! You have to be above tests/, so assuming you made this mistake, you would fix it by doing this:

```
$ cd ..    # get out of tests/
$ ls       # CORRECT! you are now in the right spot
NAME              bin            docs           setup.py        tests
$ nosetests
.
```

```
Ran 1 test in 0.004s

OK
```

Remember this because people make this mistake quite frequently.

WARNING! At the time of publication I learned that the nose project has been abandoned and might not work well. If you have strange syntax errors when you run nosetests, then look at the error output. If it references "python2.7" in the output, then chances are nosetests is trying to run the 2.7 version of Python on your computer. The solution is to run nose using python3.6 -m "nose" on Linux or macOS. On Windows you may not have this problem, but using python -m "nose" will solve it if you do.

Testing Your Setup

After you get all that installed you should be able to do this:

```
$ nosetests
.
_____

Ran 1 test in 0.007s

OK
```

I'll explain what this `nosetests` thing is doing in the next exercise, but for now if you do not see that, you probably got something wrong. Make sure you put `__init__.py` files in your NAME and `tests` directories, and make sure you got `tests/NAME_tests.py` right.

Using the Skeleton

You are now done with most of your yak shaving. Whenever you want to start a new project, just do this:

1. Make a copy of your skeleton directory. Name it after your new project.
2. Rename (move) the NAME directory to be the name of your project or whatever you want to call your root module.
3. Edit your `setup.py` to have all the information for your project.
4. Rename `tests/NAME_tests.py` to also have your module name.
5. Double check it's all working by using `nosetests` again.
6. Start coding.

Required Quiz

This exercise doesn't have Study Drills; instead, here's quiz you should complete:

1. Read about how to use all of the things you installed.
2. Read about the `setup.py` file and all it has to offer. Warning: It is not a very well-written piece of software, so it will be very strange to use.
3. Make a project and start putting code into the module, then get the module working.
4. Put a script in the `bin` directory that you can run. Read about how you can make a Python script that's runnable for your system.

5. Mention the `bin` script you created in your `setup.py` so that it gets installed.

6. Use your `setup.py` to install your own module and make sure it works, then use `pip` to uninstall it.

Common Student Questions

Do these instructions work on Windows?   They should, but depending on the version of Windows you may need to struggle with the setup a bit to get it working. Just keep researching and trying it until you get it, or see if you can ask a more experienced Python+Windows friend to help out.

What do I put in the config dictionary in my `setup.py`?   Make sure you read the documentation for `distutils` at http://docs.python.org/distutils/setupscript.html.

I can't seem to load the NAME **module and just get an** `ImportError`.   Make sure that you made the NAME/__init__.py file. If you're on Windows, make sure you didn't accidentally name it NAME/__init__.py.txt, which happens by default with some editors.

Why do we need a `bin/` **folder at all?**   This is just a standard place to put scripts that are run on the command line, not a place to put modules.

My `nosetests` **run only shows one test being run. Is that right?**   Yes, that's what my output shows, too.

Automated Testing

Having to type commands into your game over and over to make sure it's working is annoying. Wouldn't it be better to write little pieces of code that test your code? Then when you make a change, or add a new thing to your program, you just "run your tests" and the tests make sure things are still working. These automated tests won't catch all your bugs, but they will cut down on the time you spend repeatedly typing and running your code.

Every exercise after this one will not have a *What You Should See* section, but instead will have a *What You Should Test* section. You will be writing automated tests for all of your code starting now, and this will hopefully make you an even better programmer.

I won't try to explain why you should write automated tests. I will only say that you are trying to be a programmer, and programmers automate boring and tedious tasks. Testing a piece of software is definitely boring and tedious, so you might as well write a little bit of code to do it for you.

That should be all the explanation you need because *your* reason for writing unit tests is to make your brain stronger. You have gone through this book writing code to do things. Now you are going to take the next leap and write code that knows about other code you have written. This process of writing a test that runs some code you have written *forces* you to understand clearly what you have just written. It solidifies in your brain exactly what it does and why it works and gives you a new level of attention to detail.

Writing a Test Case

We're going to take a very simple piece of code and write one simple test. We're going to base this little test on a new project from your project skeleton.

First, make an ex47 project from your project skeleton. Here are the steps you should take. I'm going to give these instructions in English rather than show you how to type them so that *you* have to figure it out.

1. Copy `skeleton` to ex47.
2. Rename everything with NAME to ex47.
3. Change the word NAME in all the files to ex47.
4. Finally, remove all the `*.pyc` files to make sure you're clean.

Refer back to Exercise 46 if you get stuck, and if you can't do this easily then maybe practice it a few times.

WARNING! Remember that you run the command `nosetests` to run the tests. You can run them with `python3.6 ex47_tests.py`, but it won't work as easily, and you'll have to do it for each test file.

Next, create a simple file, `ex47/game.py`, where you can put the code to test. This will be a very silly little class that we want to test with this code in it:

game.py

```python
1  class Room(object):
2
3      def __init__(self, name, description):
4          self.name = name
5          self.description = description
6          self.paths = {}
7
8      def go(self, direction):
9          return self.paths.get(direction, None)
10
11     def add_paths(self, paths):
12         self.paths.update(paths)
```

Once you have that file, change the unit test skeleton to this:

ex47_tests.py

```python
1   from nose.tools import *
2   from ex47.game import Room
3
4
5   def test_room():
6       gold = Room("GoldRoom",
7                   """This room has gold in it you can grab. There's a
8                   door to the north.""")
9       assert_equal(gold.name, "GoldRoom")
10      assert_equal(gold.paths, {})
11
12  def test_room_paths():
13      center = Room("Center", "Test room in the center.")
14      north = Room("North", "Test room in the north.")
15      south = Room("South", "Test room in the south.")
16
17      center.add_paths({'north': north, 'south': south})
18      assert_equal(center.go('north'), north)
19      assert_equal(center.go('south'), south)
20
21  def test_map():
22      start = Room("Start", "You can go west and down a hole.")
23      west = Room("Trees", "There are trees here, you can go east.")
24      down = Room("Dungeon", "It's dark down here, you can go up.")
25
```

```
26          start.add_paths({'west': west, 'down': down})
27          west.add_paths({'east': start})
28          down.add_paths({'up': start})
29
30          assert_equal(start.go('west'), west)
31          assert_equal(start.go('west').go('east'), start)
32          assert_equal(start.go('down').go('up'), start)
```

This file imports the Room class you made in the `ex47.game` module so that you can do tests on it. There is then a set of tests that are functions starting with `test_`. Inside each test case there's a bit of code that makes a room or a set of rooms, and then makes sure the rooms work the way you expect them to work. It tests out the basic room features, then the paths, then tries out a whole map.

The important functions here are `assert_equal`, which makes sure that variables you have set or paths you have built in a Room are actually what you think they are. If you get the wrong result, then `nosetests` will print out an error message so you can go figure it out.

Testing Guidelines

Follow this loose set of guidelines when making your tests:

1. Test files go in `tests/` and are named `BLAH_tests.py`, otherwise `nosetests` won't run them. This also keeps your tests from clashing with your other code.

2. Write one test file for each module you make.

3. Keep your test cases (functions) short, but do not worry if they are a bit messy. Test cases are usually kind of messy.

4. Even though test cases are messy, try to keep them clean and remove any repetitive code you can. Create helper functions that get rid of duplicate code. You will thank me later when you make a change and then have to change your tests. Duplicated code will make changing your tests more difficult.

5. Finally, do not get too attached to your tests. Sometimes, the best way to redesign something is to just delete it and start over.

What You Should See

```
$ nosetests
...
----------------------------------------------------------------------
Ran 3 tests in 0.008s

OK
```

That's what you should see if everything is working right. Try causing an error to see what that looks like and then fix it.

Study Drills

1.   Go read about `nosetests` more, and also read about alternatives.

2.   Learn about Python's "doc tests," and see if you like them better.

3.   Make your room more advanced, and then use it to rebuild your game yet again, but this time unit test as you go.

Common Student Questions

I get a syntax error when I run `nosetests`.   If you get that then look at what the error says, and fix that line of code or the ones above it. Tools like `nosetests` are running your code and the test code, so they will find syntax errors the same as running Python will.

I can't import `ex47.game`.   Make sure you create the `ex47/__init__.py` file. Refer to Exercise 46 again to see how it's done. If that's not the problem, then do this on macOS/Linux:

```
export PYTHONPATH=.
```

And on Windows:

```
$env:PYTHONPATH = "$env:PYTHONPATH;."
```

Finally, make sure you're running the tests with `nosetests`, not with just Python.

I get `UserWarning` **when I run** `nosetests`.   You probably have two versions of Python installed, or you aren't using `distribute`. Go back and install `distribute` or `pip` as I describe in Exercise 46.

Advanced User Input

In past games you handled the user's input by simply expecting set strings. If the user typed "run," and exactly "run," then the game worked. If they typed in similar phrases like "run fast" it would fail. What we need is a device that lets users type phrases in various ways and then convert that into something the computer understands. For example, we'd like to have all of these phrases work the same:

- open door
- open the door
- go THROUGH the door
- punch bear
- Punch The Bear in the FACE

It should be alright for a user to write something a lot like English for your game and have your game figure out what it means. To do this, we're going to write a module that does just that. This module will have a few classes that work together to handle user input and convert it into something your game can work with reliably.

A simplified version of the English language could include the following elements:

- Words separated by spaces
- Sentences composed of the words
- Grammar that structures the sentences into meaning

That means the best place to start is figuring out how to get words from the user and what kinds of words those are.

Our Game Lexicon

In our game we have to create a list of allowable words called a "lexicon":

- Direction words: north, south, east, west, down, up, left, right, back
- Verbs: go, stop, kill, eat
- Stop words: the, in, of, from, at, it
- Nouns: door, bear, princess, cabinet
- Numbers: any string of 0 through 9 characters

When we get to nouns, we have a slight problem since each room could have a different set of nouns, but let's just pick this small set to work with for now and improve it later.

Breaking Up a Sentence

Once we have our lexicon we need a way to break up sentences so that we can figure out what they are. In our case, we've defined a sentence as "words separated by spaces," so we really just need to do this:

```
stuff = input('> ')
words = stuff.split()
```

That's all we'll worry about for now, but this will work really well for quite a while.

Lexicon Tuples

Once we know how to break up a sentence into words, we just have to go through the list of words and figure out what "type" they are. To do that we're going to use a handy little Python structure called a "tuple." A tuple is nothing more than a list that you can't modify. It's created by putting data inside a set of parentheses with a comma, like a list:

```
first_word = ('verb', 'go')
second_word = ('direction', 'north')
third_word = ('direction', 'west')
sentence = [first_word, second_word, third_word]
```

This creates a pair (TYPE, WORD) that lets you look at the word and do things with it.

This is just an example, but that's basically the end result. You want to take raw input from the user, carve it into words with `split`, analyze those words to identify their types, and finally, make a sentence out of them.

Scanning Input

Now you are ready to write your scanner. This scanner will take a string of raw input from a user and return a sentence that's composed of a list of tuples with the (TOKEN, WORD) pairings. If a word isn't part of the lexicon, then it should still return the WORD but set the TOKEN to an error token. These error tokens will tell users they messed up.

Here's where it gets fun. I'm not going to tell you how to do this. Instead I'm going to write a "unit test," and you are going to write the scanner so that the unit test works.

Exceptions and Numbers

There is one tiny thing I will help you with first, and that's converting numbers. In order to do this, though, we're going to cheat and use exceptions. An exception is an error that you get from some function you may have run. What happens is your function "raises" an exception when it encounters an error, then you have to handle that exception. For example, if you type this into Python you get an exception:

Exercise 48 Python Session

```
Python 3.6.0 (default, Feb  2 2017, 12:48:29)
[GCC 4.2.1 Compatible Apple LLVM 7.0.2 (clang-700.1.81)] on darwin
Type "help", "copyright", "credits" or "license" for more information.
>>> int("hell")
Traceback (most recent call last):
  File "<stdin>", line 1, in <module>
ValueError: invalid literal for int() with base 10: 'hell'
```

That ValueError is an exception that the int() function threw because what you handed int() is not a number. The int()) function could have returned a value to tell you it had an error, but since it only returns integers, it'd have a hard time doing that. It can't return -1 since that's a number. Instead of trying to figure out what to return when there's an error, the int() function raises the ValueError exception and you deal with it.

You deal with an exception by using the try and except keywords:

ex48_convert.py

```
1    def convert_number(s):
2        try:
3            return int(s)
4        except ValueError:
5            return None
```

You put the code you want to "try" inside the try block, and then you put the code to run for the error inside the except. In this case, we want to "try" to call int() on something that might be a number. If that has an error, then we "catch" it and return None.

In your scanner that you write, you should use this function to test whether something is a number. You should also do it as the last thing you check for before declaring that word an error word.

A Test First Challenge

Test first is a programming tactic where you write an automated test that pretends the code works, *then* you write the code to make the test actually work. This method works when you can't visualize how the code is implemented, but you can imagine how you have to work with it. For example, if you know how you need to use a new class in another module, but you don't quite know how to implement that class yet, then write the test first.

You are going to take a test I give you and use it to write the code that makes it work. To do this exercise, follow this procedure:

1. Create one small part of the test I give you.

2. Make sure it runs and *fails* so you know that the test is actually confirming a feature works.

3. Go to your source file, lexicon.py, and write the code that makes this test pass.

4. Repeat until you have implemented everything in the test.

When you get to step 3 it's also good to combine our other method of writing code:

1. Make the "skeleton" function or class that you need.

2. Write comments inside describing how that function works.

3. Write the code that does what the comments describe.

4. Remove any comments that just repeat the code.

This method of writing code is called "psuedo code" and works well if you don't know how to implement something, but you can describe it in your own words.

Combining the "test first" with the "psuedo code" tactics, we have this simple process for programming:

1. Write a bit of test that fails.

2. Write the skeleton function/module/class the test needs.

3. Fill the skeleton with comments in your own words explaining how it works.

4. Replace the comments with code until the test passes.

5. Repeat.

In this exercise you will practice this method of working by making a test I give you run against the lexicon.py module.

What You Should Test

Here is the test case, tests/lexicon_tests.py, that you should use, but *don't type this in yet*:

lexicon_tests.py

```
1    from nose.tools import *
2    from ex48 import lexicon
3
4
5    def test_directions():
6        assert_equal(lexicon.scan("north"), [('direction', 'north')])
7        result = lexicon.scan("north south east")
```

```
 8          assert_equal(result, [('direction', 'north'),
 9                                ('direction', 'south'),
10                                ('direction', 'east')]])
11
12      def test_verbs():
13          assert_equal(lexicon.scan("go"), [('verb', 'go')])
14          result = lexicon.scan("go kill eat")
15          assert_equal(result, [('verb', 'go'),
16                                ('verb', 'kill'),
17                                ('verb', 'eat')])
18
19
20      def test_stops():
21          assert_equal(lexicon.scan("the"), [('stop', 'the')])
22          result = lexicon.scan("the in of")
23          assert_equal(result, [('stop', 'the'),
24                                ('stop', 'in'),
25                                ('stop', 'of')])
26
27
28      def test_nouns():
29          assert_equal(lexicon.scan("bear"), [('noun', 'bear')])
30          result = lexicon.scan("bear princess")
31          assert_equal(result, [('noun', 'bear'),
32                                ('noun', 'princess')])
33
34      def test_numbers():
35          assert_equal(lexicon.scan("1234"), [('number', 1234)])
36          result = lexicon.scan("3 91234")
37          assert_equal(result, [('number', 3),
38                                ('number', 91234)])
39
40
41      def test_errors():
42          assert_equal(lexicon.scan("ASDFADFASDF"),
43                        [('error', 'ASDFADFASDF')])
44          result = lexicon.scan("bear IAS princess")
45          assert_equal(result, [('noun', 'bear'),
46                                ('error', 'IAS'),
47                                ('noun', 'princess')])
```

You will want to create a new project using the project skeleton just like you did in Exercise 47. Then you'll need to create this test case and the lexicon.py file it will use. Look at the top of the test case to see how it's being imported to figure out where it goes.

Next, follow the procedure I gave you and write a little bit of the test case at a time. For example, here's how I'd do it:

1. Write the import at the top. Get that to work.

2. Create an empty version of the first test case test_directions. Make sure that runs.

3. Write the first line of the `test_directions` test case. Make it fail.

4. Go to the `lexicon.py` file, and create an empty `scan` function.

5. Run the test, and make sure `scan` is at least running, even though it fails.

6. Fill in psuedo code comments for how `scan` should work to make `test_directions` pass.

7. Write the code that matches the comments until `test_directions` passes.

8. Go back to `test_directions` and write the rest of the lines.

9. Go back to `scan` in `lexicon.py` and work on it to make this new test code pass.

10. Once you've done that you have your first passing test, and you move on to the next test.

As long as you keep following this procedure one little chunk at a time you can successfully turn a large problem into smaller solvable problems. It's like climbing a mountain by turning it into a bunch of little hills.

Study Drills

1. Improve the unit test to make sure you test more of the lexicon.

2. Add to the lexicon and then update the unit test.

3. Make sure your scanner handles user input in any capitalization and case. Update the test to make sure this actually works.

4. Find another way to convert the number.

5. My solution was 37 lines long. Is yours longer? Shorter?

Common Student Questions

Why do I keep getting `ImportErrors`? Import errors are usually caused by four things. 1. You didn't make an `__init__.py` in a directory that has modules in it. 2. You are in the wrong directory. 3. You are importing the wrong module because you spelled it wrong. 4. Your PYTHONPATH isn't set to `.`, so you can't load modules from your current directory.

What's the difference between `try-except` **and** `if-else`? The `try-except` construct is only used for handling exceptions that modules can throw. It should *never* be used as an alternative to `if-else`.

Is there a way to keep the game running while the user is waiting to type? I'm assuming you want to have a monster attack users if they don't react quickly enough. It is possible, but it involves modules and techniques that are outside of this book's domain.

Making Sentences

What we should be able to get from our little game lexicon scanner is a list that looks like this:

```
Python 3.6.0 (default, Feb  2 2017, 12:48:29)
[GCC 4.2.1 Compatible Apple LLVM 7.0.2 (clang-700.1.81)] on darwin
Type "help", "copyright", "credits" or "license" for more information.
>>> from ex48 import lexicon
>>> lexicon.scan("go north")
[('verb', 'go'), ('direction', 'north')]
>>> lexicon.scan("kill the princess")
[('verb', 'kill'), ('stop', 'the'), ('noun', 'princess')]
>>> lexicon.scan("eat the bear")
[('verb', 'eat'), ('stop', 'the'), ('noun', 'bear')]
```

This will also work on longer sentences such as lexicon.scan("open the door and smack the bear in the nose").

Now let us turn this into something the game can work with, which would be some kind of Sentence class. If you remember grade school, a sentence can be a simple structure like:

Subject Verb Object

Obviously it gets more complex than that, and you probably did many days of annoying sentence diagrams for English class. What we want is to turn the preceding lists of tuples into a nice Sentence object that has subject, verb, and object.

Match and Peek

To do this we need five tools:

1. A way to loop through the list of scanned words. That's easy.

2. A way to "match" different types of tuples that we expect in our Subject Verb Object setup.

3. A way to "peek" at a potential tuple so we can make some decisions.

4. A way to "skip" things we do not care about, like stop words.

5. A Sentence object to put the results in.

We will be putting these functions in a module named ex48.parser in a file named ex48/parser.py in order to test it. We use the peek function to say "look at the next element in our tuple list, and then match to take one off and work with it."

The Sentence Grammar

Before you can write the code you need to understand how basic English sentence grammar works. In our parser we want to produce a Sentence object that has three attributes:

Sentence.subject   This is the subject of any sentence but could default to "player" most of the time since a sentence of "run north" is implying "player run north." This will be a noun.

Sentence.verb   This is the action of the sentence. In "run north" it would be "run." This will be a verb.

Sentence.object   This is another noun that refers to what the verb is done on. In our game we separate out directions, which would also be objects. In "run north" the word "north" would be the object. In "hit bear" the word "bear" would be the object.

Our parser then has to use the functions we described and, given a scanned sentence, convert it into an List of Sentence objects to match the input.

A Word on Exceptions

You briefly learned about exceptions but not how to raise them. This code demonstrates how to do that with the ParserError at the top. Notice that it uses classes to give it the type of Exception. Also notice the use of the raise keyword to raise the exception.

In your tests, you will want to work with these exceptions, which I'll show you how to do.

The Parser Code

If you want an extra challenge, stop right now and try to write this based on just my description. If you get stuck you can come back and see how I did it, but trying to implement the parser yourself is good practice. I will now walk through the code so you can enter it into your ex48/parser.py. We start the parser with the exception we need for a parsing error:

parser.py

```
1    class ParserError(Exception):
2        pass
```

This is how you make your own `ParserError` exception class you can throw. Next we need the Sentence object we'll create:

parser.py

```
1    class Sentence(object):
2
3        def __init__(self, subject, verb, obj):
4            # remember we take ('noun','princess') tuples and convert them
5            self.subject = subject[1]
6            self.verb = verb[1]
7            self.object = obj[1]
```

There's nothing special about this code so far. You're just making simple classes.

In our description of the problem we need a function that can peek at a list of words and return what type of word it is:

parser.py

```
1    def peek(word_list):
2        if word_list:
3            word = word_list[0]
4            return word[0]
5        else:
6            return None
```

We need this function because we'll have to make decisions about what kind of sentence we're dealing with based on what the next word is. Then we can call another function to consume that word and carry on.

To consume a word we use the `match` function, which confirms that the expected word is the right type, takes it off the list, and returns the word.

parser.py

```
1    def match(word_list, expecting):
2        if word_list:
3            word = word_list.pop(0)
4
5            if word[0] == expecting:
6                return word
7            else:
8                return None
9        else:
10            return None
```

Again, this is fairly simple, but make sure you understand this code. Also make sure you understand *why* I'm doing it this way. I need to peek at words in the list to decide what kind of sentence I'm dealing with, and then I need to match those words to create my `Sentence`.

The last thing I need is a way to skip words that aren't useful to the Sentence. These are the words labeled "stop words" (type 'stop') that are words like "the," "and," and "a."

parser.py

```
1    def skip(word_list, word_type):
2        while peek(word_list) == word_type:
3            match(word_list, word_type)
```

Remember that skip doesn't skip one word, it skips as many words of that type as it finds. This makes it so if someone types, "scream at the bear" you get "scream" and "bear."

That's our basic set of parsing functions, and with that we can actually parse just about any text we want. Our parser is very simple though, so the remaining functions are short.

First we can handle parsing a verb:

parser.py

```
1    def parse_verb(word_list):
2        skip(word_list, 'stop')
3
4        if peek(word_list) == 'verb':
5            return match(word_list, 'verb')
6        else:
7            raise ParserError("Expected a verb next.")
```

We skip any stop words, then peek ahead to make sure the next word is a "verb" type. If it's not, then raise the ParserError to say why. If it is a "verb," then match it, which takes it off the list. A similar function handles sentence objects:

parser.py

```
1    def parse_object(word_list):
2        skip(word_list, 'stop')
3        next_word = peek(word_list)
4
5        if next_word == 'noun':
6            return match(word_list, 'noun')
7        elif next_word == 'direction':
8            return match(word_list, 'direction')
9        else:
10           raise ParserError("Expected a noun or direction next.")
```

Again, skip the stop words, peek ahead, and decide if the sentence is correct based on what's there. In the parse_object function, though, we need to handle both "noun" and "direction" words as possible objects. Subjects are then similar again, but since we want to handle the implied "player" noun, we have to use peek:

```
1    def parse_subject(word_list):
2        skip(word_list, 'stop')
3        next_word = peek(word_list)
4
5        if next_word == 'noun':
6            return match(word_list, 'noun')
7        elif next_word == 'verb':
8            return ('noun', 'player')
9        else:
10           raise ParserError("Expected a verb next.")
```

With that all out of the way and ready, our final `parse_sentence` function is very simple:

```
1    def parse_sentence(word_list):
2        subj = parse_subject(word_list)
3        verb = parse_verb(word_list)
4        obj = parse_object(word_list)
5
6        return Sentence(subj, verb, obj)
```

Playing with the Parser

To see how this works, you can play with it like this:

```
Python 3.6.0 (default, Feb  2 2017, 12:48:29)
[GCC 4.2.1 Compatible Apple LLVM 7.0.2 (clang-700.1.81)] on darwin
Type "help", "copyright", "credits" or "license" for more information.
>>> from ex48.parser import *
>>> x = parse_sentence([('verb', 'run'), ('direction', 'north')])
>>> x.subject
'player'
>>> x.verb
'run'
>>> x.object
'north'
>>> x = parse_sentence([('noun', 'bear'), ('verb', 'eat'), ('stop', 'the'),
...                     ('noun', 'honey')])
>>> x.subject
'bear'
>>> x.verb
'eat'
>>> x.object
'honey'
```

Try to map sentences to the correct pairings in a sentence. For example, how would you say, "the bear run south"?

What You Should Test

For Exercise 49, write a complete test that confirms everything in this code is working. Put the test in `tests/parser_tests.py` similar to the test file from the last exercise. That includes making exceptions happen by giving the parser bad sentences.

Check for an exception by using the function `assert_raises` from the `nose` documentation. Learn how to use this so you can write a test that is *expected* to fail, which is very important in testing. Learn about this function (and others) by reading the `nose` documentation.

When you are done, you should know how this bit of code works and how to write a test for other people's code even if they do not want you to. Trust me, it's a very handy skill to have.

Study Drills

1. Change the `parse_` methods and try to put them into a class rather than use them just as methods. Which design do you like better?

2. Make the parser more error-resistant so that you can avoid annoying your users if they type words your lexicon doesn't understand.

3. Improve the grammar by handling more things like numbers.

4. Think about how you might use this `Sentence` class in your game to do more fun things with a user's input.

Common Student Questions

I can't seem to make `assert_raises` **work right.** Make sure you are writing `assert_raises(exception, callable, parameters)` and *not* writing `assert_raises(exception, callable(parameters))`. Notice how the second form is calling the function, then passing the result to `assert_raises`, which is *wrong*. You have to pass the function to call *and* its arguments to `assert_raises`.

Your First Website

These final three exercises will be very hard and you should take your time with them. In this first one you'll build a simple web version of one of your games. Before you attempt this exercise you *must* have completed Exercise 46 successfully and have a working `pip` installed such that you can install packages and know how to make a skeleton project directory. If you don't remember how to do this, go back to Exercise 46 and do it all over again.

Installing `flask`

Before creating your first web application, you'll first need to install the "web framework" called `flask`. The term "framework" generally means "some package that makes it easier for me to do something." In the world of web applications, people create "web frameworks" to compensate for the difficult problems they've encountered when making their own sites. They share these common solutions in the form of a package you can download to bootstrap your own projects.

In our case, we'll be using the `flask` framework, but there are many, many, *many* others you can choose from. For now, learn `flask`, then branch out to another one when you're ready (or just keep using `flask` since it's good enough).

Using `pip`, install `flask`:

```
$ sudo pip install flask
[sudo] password for zedshaw:
Downloading/unpacking flask
  Running setup.py egg_info for package flask

Installing collected packages: flask
  Running setup.py install for flask

Successfully installed flask
Cleaning up...
```

This will work on Linux and macOS computers, but on Windows just drop the `sudo` part of the `pip install` command and it should work. If not, go back to Exercise 46 and make sure you can do it reliably.

Make a Simple "Hello World" Project

Now you're going to make an initial very simple "Hello World" web application and project directory using `flask`. First, make your project directory:

```
$ cd projects
$ mkdir gothonweb
$ cd gothonweb
$ mkdir bin gothonweb tests docs templates
$ touch gothonweb/__init__.py
$ touch tests/__init__.py
```

You'll be taking the game from Exercise 43 and making it into a web application, so that's why you're calling it gothonweb. Before you do that, we need to create the most basic flask application possible. Put the following code into app.py:

ex50.py

```
 1    from flask import Flask
 2    app = Flask(__name__)
 3
 4    @app.route('/')
 5    def hello_world():
 6        greeting = "World"
 7        return 'Hello, {greeting}!'
 8
 9    if __name__ == "__main__":
10        app.run()
```

Then run the application like this:

```
(lpthw) $ python3.6 app.py
 * Running on http://127.0.0.1:5000/ (Press CTRL+C to quit)
```

Finally, use your web browser and go to http://localhost:5000/, and you should see two things. First, in your browser you'll see Hello, world!. Second, you'll see your Terminal with new output like this:

```
(lpthw) $ python3.6 app.py
 * Running on http://127.0.0.1:5000/ (Press CTRL+C to quit)
127.0.0.1 - - [22/Feb/2017 14:28:50] "GET / HTTP/1.1" 200 -
127.0.0.1 - - [22/Feb/2017 14:28:50] "GET /favicon.ico HTTP/1.1" 404 -
127.0.0.1 - - [22/Feb/2017 14:28:50] "GET /favicon.ico HTTP/1.1" 404 -
```

Those are log messages that flask prints out so you can see that the server is working and what the browser is doing behind the scenes. The log messages help you debug and figure out when you have problems. For example, it's saying that your browser tried to get /favicon.ico but that file didn't exist, so it returned the 404 Not Found status code.

I haven't explained the way *any* of this web stuff works yet, because I want to get you set up and ready to roll so that I can explain it better in the next two exercises. To accomplish this, I'll have you break your flask application in various ways and then restructure it so that you know how it's set up.

What's Going On?

Here's what's happening when your browser hits your application:

1. Your browser makes a network connection to your own computer, which is called `localhost` and is a standard way of saying "whatever my own computer is called on the network." It also uses port 5000.

2. Once it connects, it makes an HTTP request to the `app.py` application and asks for the / URL, which is commonly the first URL on any website.

3. Inside `app.py` you've got a list of URLs and what functions they match. The only one we have is the `'/'`, `'index'` mapping. This means that whenever someone goes to / with a browser, `flask` will find the `def index` and run it to handle the request.

4. Now that `flask` has found `def index`, it calls it to actually handle the request. This function runs and simply returns a string for what `flask` should send to the browser.

5. Finally, `flask` has handled the request and sends this response to the browser, which is what you are seeing.

Make sure you really understand this. Draw up a diagram of how this information flows from your browser, to `flask`, then to `def index` and back to your browser.

Fixing Errors

First, delete line 5 where you assign the `greeting` variable, then hit refresh in your browser. Then use CTRL-C to kill `flask` and start it again. Once it's running again refresh your browser, and you should see an "Internal Server Error." Back in your Terminal you'll see this ([VENV] is the path to your `.venvs/` directory):

```
(lpthw) $ python3.6 app.py
 * Running on http://127.0.0.1:5000/ (Press CTRL+C to quit)
[2017-02-22 14:35:54,256] ERROR in app: Exception on / [GET]
Traceback (most recent call last):
  File "[VENV]/site-packages/flask/app.py",
    line 1982, in wsgi_app
    response = self.full_dispatch_request()
  File "[VENV]/site-packages/flask/app.py",
    line 1614, in full_dispatch_request
    rv = self.handle_user_exception(e)
  File "[VENV]/site-packages/flask/app.py",
    line 1517, in handle_user_exception
    reraise(exc_type, exc_value, tb)
  File "[VENV]/site-packages/flask/_compat.py",
    line 33, in reraise
    raise value
```

```
   File "[VENV]/site-packages/flask/app.py",
 line 1612, in full_dispatch_request
      rv = self.dispatch_request()
   File "[VENV]/site-packages/flask/app.py",
 line 1598, in dispatch_request
      return self.view_functions[rule.endpoint](**req.view_args)
   File "app.py", line 8, in index
      return render_template("index.html", greeting=greeting)
 NameError: name 'greeting' is not defined
 127.0.0.1 — — [22/Feb/2017 14:35:54] "GET / HTTP/1.1" 500 —
```

This works well enough, but you can also run `flask` in "debugger mode." This will give you a better error page and more useful information. The problem with debugger mode is it's not safe to run on the internet, so you have to explicitly turn it on like this:

```
(lpthw) $ export FLASK_DEBUG=1
(lpthw) $ python3.6 app.py
 * Running on http://127.0.0.1:5000/ (Press CTRL+C to quit)
 * Restarting with stat
 * Debugger is active!
 * Debugger pin code: 222—752—342
```

After this, you hit refresh in your browser, and you get a much more detailed page with information you can use to debug the application and a live console to work with to find out more.

WARNING! It's the `flask` live debugging console and the improved output that makes debug mode so dangerous on the internet. With this information an attacker can completely control your machine remotely. If you ever do place your web application on the internet do *not* activate debugger mode. In fact, I would avoid making FLASK_DEBUG easy to activate. It's tempting to simply hack this startup so that you save a step during development, but then that hack will get onto your web server and it'll turn into a real hack, not just something lazy you did one night when you were tired.

Create Basic Templates

You can break your `flask` application, but did you notice that "Hello World" isn't a very good HTML page? This is a web application, and as such it needs a proper HTML response. To do that you will create a simple template that says "Hello World" in a big green font.

The first step is to create a `templates/index.html` file that looks like this:

index.html

```
<html>
    <head>
```

```
        <title>Gothons Of Planet Percal #25</title>
    </head>
<body>

{% if greeting %}
    I just wanted to say
    <em style="color: green; font-size: 2em;">{{ greeting }}</em>.
{% else %}
    <em>Hello</em>, world!
{% endif %}

</body>
</html>
```

If you know what HTML is, then this should look fairly familiar. If not, research HTML and try writing a few web pages by hand so you know how it works. This HTML file, however, is a template, which means that flask will fill in "holes" in the text depending on variables you pass in to the template. Every place you see {{ greeting }} will be a variable you'll pass to the template that alters its contents.

To make your app.py do this, you need to add some code to tell flask where to load the template and to render it. Take that file and change it like this:

app.py

```
1    from flask import Flask
2    from flask import render_template
3
4    app = Flask(__name__)
5
6    @app.route("/")
7    def index():
8        greeting = "Hello World"
9        return render_template("index.html", greeting=greeting)
10
11   if __name__ == "__main__":
12       app.run()
```

Once you have that in place, reload the web page in your browser, and you should see a different message in green. You should also be able to do a View Source on the page in your browser to see that it is valid HTML.

This may have flown by you very fast, so let me explain how a template works:

1.   In your app.py you've imported a new function named render_template at the top.

2.   This render_template knows how to load .html files out of the templates/ directory, because that is the default magic setting for a flask application.

3. Later in your code, when the browser hits the `def index`, instead of just returning the string `greeting`, you call `render_template` and pass the greeting to it as a variable.

4. This `render_template` method then loads the `templates/index.html` file (even though you didn't explicitly say `templates`) and processes it.

5. In this `templates/index.html` file you have what looks like normal HTML, but then there's "code" placed between two kinds of markers. One is `{% %}`, which marks pieces of "executable code" (if-statements, for-loops, etc.). The other is `{{ }}`, which marks variables to be converted into text and placed into the HTML output. The `{% %}` executable code doesn't show up in the HTML. To learn more about this template language read the Jinja2 documentation.

To get deeper into this, change the greeting variable and the HTML to see what effect it has. Also create another template named `templates/foo.html` and render that like before.

Study Drills

1. Read the documentation at http://flask.pocoo.org/docs/0.12/, which is the same as the `flask` project.

2. Experiment with everything you can find there, including their example code.

3. Read about HTML5 and CSS3 and make some other .html and .css files for practice.

4. If you have a friend who knows Django and is willing to help you, then consider doing Exercises 50, 51, and 52 in Django instead to see what that's like.

Common Student Questions

I can't seem to connect to `http://localhost:5000/`. Try `http://127.0.0.1:5000/` instead.

I can't find `index.html` **(or just about anything).** You probably are doing `cd bin/` first and then trying to work with the project. Do not do this. All of the commands and instructions assume you are one directory above `bin/`, so if you can't type `python3.6 app.py` then you are in the wrong directory.

Why do we assign `greeting=greeting` **when we call the template?** You are not assigning to `greeting`. You are setting a named parameter to give to the template. It's sort of an assignment, but it only affects the call to the template function.

I can't use port 5000 on my computer. You probably have an anti-virus program installed that is using that port. Try a different port.

Getting Input from a Browser

W hile it's exciting to see the browser display "Hello World," it's even more exciting to let the user submit text to your application from a form. In this exercise we'll improve our starter web application by using forms and storing information about users into their "sessions."

How the Web Works

Time for some boring stuff. You need to understand a bit more about how the web works before you can make a form. This description isn't complete, but it's accurate and will help you figure out what might be going wrong with your application. Also, creating forms will be easier if you know what they do.

I'll start with a simple diagram that shows you the different parts of a web request and how the information flows:

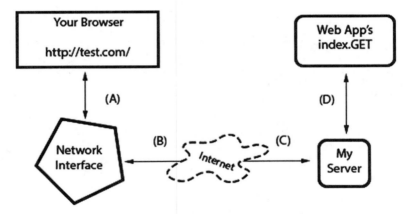

I've labeled the lines with letters so I can walk you through a regular request process:

1. You type in the url http://test.com// into your browser, and it sends the request on line (A) to your computer's network interface.

2. Your request goes out over the internet on line (B) and then to the remote computer on line (C) where my server accepts the request.

3. Once my computer accepts it, my web application gets it on line (D), and my Python code runs the index.GET handler.

4. The response comes out of my Python server when I return it, and it goes back to your browser over line (D) again.

5. The server running this site takes the response off `line (D)`, then sends it back over the internet on `line (C)`.

6. The response from the server then comes off the internet on `line (B)`, and your computer's network interface hands it to your browser on `line (A)`.

7. Finally, your browser then displays the response.

In this description there are a few terms you should know so that you have a common vocabulary to work with when talking about your web application:

Browser   The software that you're probably using every day. Most people don't know what a browser really does. They just call browsers "the internet." Its job is to take addresses (like http://test.com/) you type into the URL bar, then use that information to make requests to the server at that address.

Address   This is normally a URL (Uniform Resource Locator) like http://test.com/ and indicates where a browser should go. The first part, `http`, indicates the protocol you want to use, in this case "Hyper-Text Transport Protocol." You can also try ftp://ibiblio.org/ to see how "File Transport Protocol" works. The http://test.com/ part is the "hostname," a human readable address you can remember and which maps to a number called an IP address, similar to a telephone number for a computer on the internet. Finally, URLs can have a trailing `path` like the /book/ part of http://test.com/book/, which indicates a file or some resource *on* the server to retrieve with a request. There are many other parts, but those are the main ones.

Connection   Once a browser knows what protocol you want to use (http), what server you want to talk to (http://test.com/), and what resource on that server to get, it must make a connection. The browser simply asks your operating system (OS) to open a "port" to the computer, usually port 80. When it works, the OS hands back to your program something that works like a file, but is actually sending and receiving bytes over the network wires between your computer and the other computer at http://test.com/. This is also the same thing that happens with http://localhost:8080/, but in this case you're telling the browser to connect to your own computer (localhost) and use port 8080 rather than the default of 80. You could also do http://test.com:80/ and get the same result, except you're explicitly saying to use port 80 instead of letting it be that by default.

Request   Your browser is connected using the address you gave. Now it needs to ask for the resource it wants (or you want) on the remote server. If you gave /book/ at the end of the URL, then you want the file (resource) at `/book/`, and most servers will use the real file `/book/index.html` but pretend it doesn't exist. What the browser does to get this resource is send a *request* to the server. I won't get into exactly how it does this, but just understand that it has to send something to query the server for the request. The interesting thing is that these "resources" don't have to be files. For instance, when the browser in your application asks for something, the server is returning something your Python code generated.

Server   The server is the computer at the end of a browser's connection that knows how to answer your browser's requests for files/resources. Most web servers just send files, and that's actually the majority of traffic. But you're actually building a server in Python that knows how to take requests for resources and then return strings that you craft using Python. When you do this crafting, *you* are pretending to be a file to the browser, but really it's just code. As you can see from Exercise 50, it also doesn't take much code to create a response.

Response   This is the HTML (CSS, JavaScript, or images) your server wants to send back to the browser as the answer to the browser's request. In the case of files, it just reads them off the disk and sends them to the browser, but it wraps the contents of the disk in a special "header" so the browser knows what it's getting. In the case of your application, you're still sending the same thing, including the header, but you generate that data on the fly with your Python code.

That is the fastest crash course in how a web browser accesses information on servers on the internet. It should work well enough for you to understand this exercise, but if not, read about it as much as you can until you get it. A really good way to do that is to take the diagram and break different parts of the web application you did in Exercise 50. If you can break your web application in predictable ways using the diagram, you'll start to understand how it works.

How Forms Work

The best way to play with forms is to write some code that accepts form data, and then see what you can do. Take your `app.py` file and make it look like this:

form_test.py

```
1   from flask import Flask
2   from flask import render_template
3   from flask import request
4
5   app = Flask(__name__)
6
7   @app.route("/hello")
8   def index():
9       name = request.args.get('name', 'Nobody')
10
11      if name:
12          greeting = f"Hello, {name}"
13      else:
14          greeting = "Hello World"
15
16      return render_template("index.html", greeting=greeting)
17
18  if __name__ == "__main__":
19      app.run()
```

Restart it (hit CTRL-C and then run it again) to make sure it loads again, then with your browser go to `http://localhost:5000/hello`, which should display, "I just wanted to say Hello, Nobody." Next, change the URL in your browser to `http://localhost:5000/hello?name=Frank`, and you'll see it say, "Hello, Frank." Finally, change the `name=Frank` part to be your name. Now it's saying hello to you.

Let's break down the changes I made to your script.

1. Instead of just a string for `greeting`, I'm now using `request.args` to get data from the browser. This is a simple `dict` that contains the form values as key=value pairs.

2. I then construct the `greeting` from the new name, which should be very familiar to you by now.

3. Everything else about the file is the same as before.

You're also not restricted to just one parameter on the URL. Change this example to give two variables like this: `http://localhost:5000/hello?name=Frank&greet=Hola`. Then change the code to get name and greet like this:

```
greet = request.args.get('greet', 'Hello')
greeting = f"{greet}, {name}"
```

You should also try *not* giving the greet and name parameters on the URL. You'll simply send your browser to `http://localhost:5000/hello` to see that the `index` now defaults to "Nobody" for name and "Hello" for greet.

Creating HTML Forms

Passing the parameters on the URL works, but it's kind of ugly and not easy to use for regular people. What you really want is a "POST form," which is a special HTML file that has a <form> tag in it. This form will collect information from the user, then send it to your web application just like you did above.

Let's make a quick one so you can see how it works. Here's the new HTML file you need to create, in `templates/hello_form.html`:

hello_form.html

```
<html>
    <head>
        <title>Sample Web Form</title>
    </head>
<body>

<h1>Fill Out This Form</h1>
```

```
<form action="/hello" method="POST">
    A Greeting: <input type="text" name="greet">
    <br/>
    Your Name: <input type="text" name="name">
    <br/>
    <input type="submit">
</form>

</body>
</html>
```

You should then change app.py to look like this:

app.py

```
1   from flask import Flask
2   from flask import render_template
3   from flask import request
4
5   app = Flask(__name__)
6
7   @app.route("/hello", methods=['POST', 'GET'])
8   def index():
9       greeting = "Hello World"
10
11      if request.method == "POST":
12          name = request.form['name']
13          greet = request.form['greet']
14          greeting = f"{greet}, {name}"
15          return render_template("index.html", greeting=greeting)
16      else:
17          return render_template("hello_form.html")
18
19
20  if __name__ == "__main__":
21      app.run()
```

Once you've got those written up, simply restart the web application again and hit it with your browser like before.

This time you'll get a form asking you for "A Greeting" and "Your Name." When you hit the Submit button on the form, it will give you the same greeting you normally get, but this time look at the URL in your browser. See how it's http://localhost:5000/hello even though you sent in parameters.

The part of the hello_form.html file that makes this work is the line with <form action="/hello" method="POST">. This tells your browser to:

1. Collect data from the user using the form fields inside the form.

2. Send them to the server using a POST type of request, which is just another browser request that "hides" the form fields.

3. Send that to the /hello URL (as shown in the action="/hello" part).

You can then see how the two `<input>` tags match the names of the variables in your new code. Also notice that instead of just a GET method inside `class index`, I have another method, POST. How this new application works is as follows:

1. Your request goes to `index()` like normal, except now there is an `if-statement` that checks the `request.method` for either `"POST"` or `"GET"` methods. This is how the browser tells `app.py` that a request is either a form submission or URL parameters.

2. If `request.method` is `"POST"`, then you process the form as if it were filled out and submitted, returning the proper greeting.

3. If `request.method` is anything else, then you simply return the `hello_form.html` for the user to fill out.

As an exercise, go into the `templates/index.html` file and add a link *back* to just `/hello` so that you can keep filling out the form and seeing the results. Make sure you can explain how this link works and how it's letting you cycle between `templates/index.html` and `templates/hello_form.html` and what's being run inside this latest Python code.

Creating a Layout Template

When you work on your game in the next exercise, you'll need to make a bunch of little HTML pages. Writing a full web page each time will quickly become tedious. Luckily you can create a "layout" template, or a kind of shell that will wrap all your other pages with common headers and footers. Good programmers try to reduce repetition, so layouts are essential for being a good programmer.

Change `templates/index.html` to be like this:

index_laid_out.html

```
{% extends "layout.html" %}

{% block content %}

{% if greeting %}
    I just wanted to say
    <em style="color: green; font-size: 2em;">{{ greeting }}</em>.
{% else %}
    <em>Hello</em>, world!
{% endif %}

{% endblock %}
```

Then change `templates/hello_form.html` to be like this:

hello_form_laid_out.html

```
{% extends "layout.html" %}

{% block content %}
```

```
<h1>Fill Out This Form</h1>

<form action="/hello" method="POST">
    A Greeting: <input type="text" name="greet">
    <br/>
    Your Name: <input type="text" name="name">
    <br/>
    <input type="submit">
</form>

{% endblock %}
```

All we're doing is stripping out the "boilerplate" at the top and the bottom, which is always on every page. We'll put that back into a single `templates/layout.html` file that handles it for us from now on.

Once you have those changes, create a `templates/layout.html` file with this in it:

layout.html

```
<html>
<head>
    <title>Gothons From Planet Percal #25</title>
</head>
<body>

{% block content %}

{% endblock %}

</body>
</html>
```

This file looks like a regular template, except that it's going to be passed the *contents* of the other templates and used to *wrap* them. Anything you put in here doesn't need to be in the other templates. Your other HTML templates will be inserted into the `{% block content %}` section. `flask` knows to use this `layout.html` as the layout because you put `{% extends "layout.html" %}` at the top of your templates.

Writing Automated Tests for Forms

It's easy to test a web application with your browser by just hitting refresh, but come on, we're programmers here. Why do some repetitive task when we can write some code to test our application? What you're going to do next is write a little test for your web application form based on what you learned in Exercise 47. If you don't remember Exercise 47, read it again.

Create a new file named `tests/app_tests.py` with this:

```python
1    from nose.tools import *
2    from app import app
3
4    app.config['TESTING'] = True
5    web = app.test_client()
6
7    def test_index():
8        rv = web.get('/', follow_redirects=True)
9        assert_equal(rv.status_code, 404)
10
11        rv = web.get('/hello', follow_redirects=True)
12        assert_equal(rv.status_code, 200)
13        assert_in(b"Fill Out This Form", rv.data)
14
15        data = {'name': 'Zed', 'greet': 'Hola'}
16        rv = web.post('/hello', follow_redirects=True, data=data)
17        assert_in(b"Zed", rv.data)
18        assert_in(b"Hola", rv.data)
```

Finally, use `nosetests` to run this test setup and test your web application:

```
$ nosetests
.

Ran 1 test in 0.059s

OK
```

What I'm doing here is I'm actually *importing* the whole application from the `app.py` module, then running it manually. The `flask` framework has a very simple API for processing requests, which looks like this:

```python
data = {'name': 'Zed', 'greet': 'Hola'}
rv = web.post('/hello', follow_redirects=True, data=data)
```

This means you can send a POST request using the `post()` method, and then give it the form data as a `dict`. Everything else works the same as testing `web.get()` requests.

In the `tests/app_tests.py` automated test I'm first making sure the / URL returns a "404 Not Found" response, since it actually doesn't exist. Then I'm checking that /hello works with both a GET and a POST form. Following the test should be fairly simple, even if you might not totally know what's going on.

Take some time studying this latest application, especially how the automated testing works. Make sure you understand how I imported the application from app.py and ran it directly for the automated test. This is an important trick that will lead to more learning.

Study Drills

1. Read even more about HTML, and give the simple form a better layout. It helps to draw what you want to do on paper and *then* implement it with HTML.

2. This one is hard, but try to figure out how you'd do a file upload form so that you can upload an image and save it to the disk.

3. This is even more mind-numbing, but go find the HTTP RFC (which is the document that describes how HTTP works) and read as much of it as you can. It is really boring but comes in handy once in a while.

4. This will also be really difficult, but see if you can find someone to help you set up a web server like Apache, Nginx, or thttpd. Try to serve a couple of your .html and .css files with it just to see if you can. Don't worry if you can't. Web servers kind of suck.

5. Take a break after this and just try making as many different web applications as you can.

Breaking It

This is a great place to figure out how to break web applications. You should experiment with the following:

1. How much damage can you do with the FLASK_DEBUG setting on? Be careful that you don't wipe yourself out doing this.

2. Let's say you don't have default parameters for the forms. What could go wrong?

3. You're checking for POST and then "anything else." You can use the curl command line tool to generate different request types. What happens?

The Start of Your Web Game

We're coming to the end of the book, and in this exercise I'm going to really challenge you. When you're done, you'll be a reasonably competent Python beginner. You'll still need to go through a few more books and write a couple more projects, but you'll have the skills to complete them. The only obstacles will be time, motivation, and resources.

In this exercise, we won't make a complete game, but instead we'll make an "engine" that can run the game from Exercise 47 in the browser. This will involve refactoring Exercise 43, mixing in the structure from Exercise 47, adding automated tests, and finally creating a web engine that can run the games.

This exercise will be *huge*, and I predict you could spend anywhere from a week to months on it before moving on. It's best to attack it in little chunks and do a bit a night, taking your time to make everything work before moving on.

Refactoring the Exercise 43 Game

You've been altering the gothonweb project for two exercises, and you'll do it one more time in this exercise. The skill you're learning is called "refactoring," or as I like to call it, "fixing stuff." Refactoring is a term programmers use to describe the process of taking old code and changing it to have new features or just to clean it up. You've been doing this without even knowing it, as it's second nature to building software.

What you'll do in this part is take the ideas from Exercise 47 of a testable "map" of Rooms and the game from Exercise 43 and combine them together to create a new game structure. It will have the same content, just "refactored" to have a better structure.

The first step is to grab the code from ex47/game.py, copy it to gothonweb/planisphere.py, copy the tests/ex47_tests.py file to tests/planisphere_tests.py, and run nosetests again to make sure it keeps working. The word "planisphere" is just a synonym for "map," which avoids Python's built-in map function. The thesaurus is your friend.

WARNING! From now on I won't show you the output of a test run. Just assume that you should be doing it and it'll look like the preceding unless you have an error.

Once you have the code from Exercise 47 copied over, it's time to refactor it to have the Exercise 43 map in it. I'm going to start off by laying down the basic structure, and then you'll have an assignment to make the planisphere.py file and the planisphere_tests.py file complete.

Lay out the basic structure of the map using the Room class as it is now:

planisphere.py

```
 1    class Room(object):
 2
 3        def __init__(self, name, description):
 4            self.name = name
 5            self.description = description
 6            self.paths = {}
 7
 8        def go(self, direction):
 9            return self.paths.get(direction, None)
10
11        def add_paths(self, paths):
12            self.paths.update(paths)
13
14
15    central_corridor = Room("Central Corridor",
16    """
17    The Gothons of Planet Percal #25 have invaded your ship and destroyed
18    your entire crew.  You are the last surviving member and your last
19    mission is to get the neutron destruct bomb from the Weapons Armory, put
20    it in the bridge, and blow the ship up after getting into an escape pod.
21
22    You're running down the central corridor to the Weapons Armory when a
23    Gothon jumps out, red scaly skin, dark grimy teeth, and evil clown
24    costume flowing around his hate filled body.  He's blocking the door to
25    the Armory and about to pull a weapon to blast you.
26    """)
27
28
29    laser_weapon_armory = Room("Laser Weapon Armory",
30    """
31    Lucky for you they made you learn Gothon insults in the academy.  You
32    tell the one Gothon joke you know: Lbhe zbgure vf fb sng, jura fur fvgf
33    nebhaq gur ubhfr, fur fvgf nebhaq gur ubhfr.  The Gothon stops, tries
34    not to laugh, then busts out laughing and can't move.  While he's
35    laughing you run up and shoot him square in the head putting him down,
36    then jump through the Weapon Armory door.
37
38    You do a dive roll into the Weapon Armory, crouch and scan the room for
39    more Gothons that might be hiding.  It's dead quiet, too quiet.  You
40    stand up and run to the far side of the room and find the neutron bomb
41    in its container.  There's a keypad lock on the box and you need the
42    code to get the bomb out.  If you get the code wrong 10 times then the
43    lock closes forever and you can't get the bomb.  The code is 3 digits.
44    """)
45
46
47    the_bridge = Room("The Bridge",
48    """
```

```
49   The container clicks open and the seal breaks, letting gas out.  You
50   grab the neutron bomb and run as fast as you can to the bridge where you
51   must place it in the right spot.
52
53   You burst onto the Bridge with the netron destruct bomb under your arm
54   and surprise 5 Gothons who are trying to take control of the ship.  Each
55   of them has an even uglier clown costume than the last.  They haven't
56   pulled their weapons out yet, as they see the active bomb under your arm
57   and don't want to set it off.
58   """)
59
60
61   escape_pod = Room("Escape Pod",
62   """
63   You point your blaster at the bomb under your arm and the Gothons put
64   their hands up and start to sweat.  You inch backward to the door, open
65   it, and then carefully place the bomb on the floor, pointing your
66   blaster at it.  You then jump back through the door, punch the close
67   button and blast the lock so the Gothons can't get out.  Now that the
68   bomb is placed you run to the escape pod to get off this tin can.
69
70   You rush through the ship desperately trying to make it to the escape
71   pod before the whole ship explodes.  It seems like hardly any Gothons
72   are on the ship, so your run is clear of interference.  You get to the
73   chamber with the escape pods, and now need to pick one to take.  Some of
74   them could be damaged but you don't have time to look.  There's 5 pods,
75   which one do you take?
76   """)
77
78
79   the_end_winner = Room("The End",
80   """
81   You jump into pod 2 and hit the eject button.  The pod easily slides out
82   into space heading to the planet below.  As it flies to the planet, you
83   look back and see your ship implode then explode like a bright star,
84   taking out the Gothon ship at the same time.  You won!
85   """)
86
87
88   the_end_loser = Room("The End",
89   """
90   You jump into a random pod and hit the eject button.  The pod escapes
91   out into the void of space, then implodes as the hull ruptures, crushing
92   your body into jam jelly.
93   """
94   )
95
96   escape_pod.add_paths({
97       '2': the_end_winner,
98       '*': the_end_loser
```

```
 99     })
100
101     generic_death = Room("death", "You died.")
102
103     the_bridge.add_paths({
104         'throw the bomb': generic_death,
105         'slowly place the bomb': escape_pod
106     })
107
108     laser_weapon_armory.add_paths({
109         '0132': the_bridge,
110         '*': generic_death
111     })
112
113     central_corridor.add_paths({
114         'shoot!': generic_death,
115         'dodge!': generic_death,
116         'tell a joke': laser_weapon_armory
117     })
118
119     START = 'central_corridor'
120
121     def load_room(name):
122         """
123         There is a potential security problem here.
124         Who gets to set name? Can that expose a variable?
125         """
126         return globals().get(name)
127
128     def name_room(room):
129         """
130         Same possible security problem.  Can you trust room?
131         What's a better solution than this globals lookup?
132         """
133         for key, value in globals().items():
134             if value == room:
135                 return key
```

You'll notice that there are a couple of problems with our Room class and this map:

1. We have to put the text that was in the if-else clauses that got printed *before* entering a room as part of each room. This means you can't shuffle the planisphere around, which would be nice. You'll be fixing that up in this exercise.

2. There are parts in the original game where we ran code that determined things like the bomb's keypad code or the right pod. In this game we just pick some defaults and go with it, but later you'll be given Study Drills to make this work again.

3. I've just made a `generic_death` ending for all of the bad decisions, which you'll have to finish for me. You'll need to go back through and add in all the original endings and make sure they work.

4. I've got a new kind of transition labeled `"*"` that will be used for a "catch-all" action in the engine.

Once you've got that basically written out, here's the new automated test, `tests/planisphere_test.py`, that you should have to get yourself started:

planisphere_tests.py

```
1   from nose.tools import *
2   from gothonweb.planisphere import *
3
4   def test_room():
5       gold = Room("GoldRoom",
6                   """This room has gold in it you can grab. There's a
7                   door to the north.""")
8       assert_equal(gold.name, "GoldRoom")
9       assert_equal(gold.paths, {})
10
11  def test_room_paths():
12      center = Room("Center", "Test room in the center.")
13      north = Room("North", "Test room in the north.")
14      south = Room("South", "Test room in the south.")
15
16      center.add_paths({'north': north, 'south': south})
17      assert_equal(center.go('north'), north)
18      assert_equal(center.go('south'), south)
19
20  def test_map():
21      start = Room("Start", "You can go west and down a hole.")
22      west = Room("Trees", "There are trees here, you can go east.")
23      down = Room("Dungeon", "It's dark down here, you can go up.")
24
25      start.add_paths({'west': west, 'down': down})
26      west.add_paths({'east': start})
27      down.add_paths({'up': start})
28
29      assert_equal(start.go('west'), west)
30      assert_equal(start.go('west').go('east'), start)
31      assert_equal(start.go('down').go('up'), start)
32
33  def test_gothon_game_map():
34      start_room = load_room(START)
35      assert_equal(start_room.go('shoot!'), generic_death)
36      assert_equal(start_room.go('dodge!'), generic_death)
37
38      room = start_room.go('tell a joke')
39      assert_equal(room, laser_weapon_armory)
```

Your task in this part of the exercise is to complete the map and make the automated test completely validate the whole map. This includes fixing all the generic_death objects to be real endings. Make sure this works really well and that your test is as complete as possible because we'll be changing this map later, and you'll use the tests to make sure it keeps working.

Creating an Engine

You should have your game map working and a good unit test for it. I now want you to make a simple little game engine that will run the rooms, collect input from the player, and keep track of where a player is in the game. We'll be using the sessions you just learned to make a simple game engine that will do the following:

1.   Start a new game for new users.

2.   Present the room to the user.

3.   Take input from the user.

4.   Run user input through the game.

5.   Display the results and keep going until the user dies.

To do this, you're going to take the trusty app.py you've been hacking on and create a fully working, session-based game engine. The catch is I'm going to make a very simple one with *basic HTML* files, and it'll be up to you to complete it. Here's the base engine:

app.py

```
1    from flask import Flask, session, redirect, url_for, escape, request
2    from flask import render_template
3    from gothonweb import planisphere
4
5    app = Flask(__name__)
6
7    @app.route("/")
8    def index():
9        # this is used to "setup" the session with starting values
10       session['room_name'] = planisphere.START
11       return redirect(url_for("game"))
12
13   @app.route("/game", methods=['GET', 'POST'])
14   def game():
15       room_name = session.get('room_name')
16
17       if request.method == "GET":
18           if room_name:
19               room = planisphere.load_room(room_name)
20               return render_template("show_room.html", room=room)
```

```
21            else:
22                # why is there here? do you need it?'
23                return render_template("you_died.html")
24        else:
25            action = request.form.get('action')
26
27            if room_name and action:
28                room = planisphere.load_room(room_name)
29                next_room = room.go(action)
30
31                if not next_room:
32                    session['room_name'] = planisphere.name_room(room)
33                else:
34                    session['room_name'] = planisphere.name_room(next_room)
35
36            return redirect(url_for("game"))
37
38
39    # YOU SHOULD CHANGE THIS IF YOU PUT ON THE INTERNET
40    app.secret_key = 'A0Zr98j/3yX R~XHH!jmN]LWX/,?RT'
41
42    if __name__ == "__main__":
43        app.run()
```

There are even more new things in this script, but amazingly it's an entire web-based game engine in a small file. Before you run `app.py` you need to change your PYTHONPATH environment variable. Don't know what that is? I know, it's kind of dumb, but you have to learn what this is to run even basic Python programs: that's how Python people like things.

In your Terminal, type:

```
export PYTHONPATH=$PYTHONPATH:.
```

On Windows PowerShell do:

```
$env:PYTHONPATH = "$env:PYTHONPATH;."
```

You should only have to do it once per shell session, but if you get an import error, then you probably need to do this or you did it wrong.

You should next delete `templates/hello_form.html` and `templates/index.html` and create the two templates mentioned in the preceding code. Here's a *very* simple `templates/show_room.html`:

show_room.html

```
{% extends "layout.html" %}

{% block content %}

<h1> {{ room.name }}  </h1>
```

```
<pre>
{{ room.description }}
</pre>

{% if room.name in ["death", "The End"] %}
    <p><a href="/">Play Again?</a></p>
{% else %}
    <p>
    <form action="/game" method="POST">
        - <input type="text" name="action"> <input type="SUBMIT">
    </form>
    </p>
{% endif %}


{% endblock %}
```

That is the template to show a room as you travel through the game. Next you need one to tell someone they died in the case that they got to the end of the map on accident, which is `templates/you_died`
`.html`:

you_died.html

```
<h1>You Died!</h1>

<p>Looks like you bit the dust.</p>
<p><a href="/">Play Again</a></p>
```

With those in place, you should now be able to do the following:

1. Get the test `tests/app_tests.py` working again so that you are testing the game. You won't be able to do much more than a few clicks in the game because of sessions, but you should be able to do some basics.

2. Run the `python3.6 app.py` script and test out the game.

You should be able to refresh and fix the game like normal. You should also be able to work with the game HTML and engine until it does all the things you want it to do.

Your Final Exam

Do you feel like this was a huge amount of information thrown at you all at once? Good, I want you to have something to tinker with while you build your skills. To complete this exercise, I'm going to give you a final set of tasks for you to complete on your own. You'll notice that what you've written so far isn't very well built; it is just a first version of the code. Your job now is to make the game more complete by doing these things:

1. Fix all the bugs I mention in the code and any that I didn't mention. If you find new bugs, let me know.

2.   Improve all of the automated tests so that you test more of the application, and get to a point where you use a test rather than your browser to check the application while you work.

3.   Make the HTML look better.

4.   Research logins and create a signup system for the application so people can have logins and high scores.

5.   Complete the game map, making it as large and feature-complete as possible.

6.   Give people a "help" system that lets them ask what they can do at each room in the game.

7.   Add any other features you can think of to the game.

8.   Create several "maps" and let people choose a game they want to run. Your app.py engine should be able to run any map of rooms you give it, so you can support multiple games.

9.   Finally, use what you learned in Exercises 48 and 49 to create a better input processor. You have most of the code necessary; you just need to improve the grammar and hook it up to your input form and the GameEngine.

Good luck!

Common Student Questions

I'm using sessions **in my game, and I can't test it with** nosetests.   Read the Flask Testing Documentation about "Other Testing Tricks" (http://flask.pocoo.org/docs/0.12/testing/#other-testing-tricks) for information on creating fake sessions inside your tests.

I get an ImportError.   It could be one or more of these: wrong directory, wrong Python version, PYTHONPATH not set, no __init__.py file, and/or spelling mistake in import.

Next Steps

You're not a programmer quite yet. I like to think of this book as giving you your "programming black belt." You know enough to start another book on programming and handle it just fine. This book should have given you the mental tools and attitude you need to go through most Python books and actually learn something. It might even make it easy.

I recommend you check out some of these projects and try to build something with them:

- Learn Ruby The Hard Way (https://learnrubythehardway.org): You will learn even more about programming as you learn more programming languages, so try learning Ruby, too.
- The Django Tutorial (https://docs.djangoproject.com/en/1.11/intro/): Build a web application with the Django web framework.
- SciPy (https://www.scipy.org): Check this out if you're into science, math, and engineering.
- PyGame (http://www.pygame.org): Make a game with graphics and sound.
- Pandas (http://pandas.pydata.org): Use this for doing data manipulation and analysis.
- Natural Language Toolkit (http://www.nltk.org): Use this for analyzing written text and writing things like spam filters and chat bots.
- TensorFlow (https://www.tensorflow.org): Use this for machine learning and visualization.
- Requests (http://docs.python-requests.org): Learn the client side of HTTP and the web.
- ScraPy (https://scrapy.org): Try scraping some web sites to get information off them.
- Kivy (https://kivy.org): Create user interfaces on desktops and mobile platforms.
- Learn C The Hard Way (https://learncodethehardway.org): After you're familiar with Python, try learning C and algorithms with my other book. Take it slow; C is different but a very good thing to learn.

Pick one of the preceding resources, and go through any tutorials and documentation they have. As you go through documentation with code in it, *type in all of the code* and make it work. That's how I do it. That's how every programmer does it. Reading programming documentation is not enough to learn it; you have to do it. After you get through the tutorial and any other cocumentation they have, make something. Anything will do, even something someone else has already written. Just make something.

Just understand anything you write will probably suck. That's alright, though; I suck at every programming language at first. Nobody writes pure perfect gold when they're a beginner, and anyone who tells you they did is a huge liar.

How to Learn Any Programming Language

I'm going to teach you how to learn most of the programming languages you may want to learn in the future. The organization of this book is based on how I and many other programmers learn new languages. The process that I usually follow is as follows:

1. Get a book or some introductory text about the language.

2. Go through the book and type in all of the code, making all of it run.

3. Read the book as you work on the code, taking notes.

4. Use the language to implement a small set of programs you are familiar with in another language.

5. Read other people's code in the language, and try to copy their patterns.

In this book, I forced you to go through this process very slowly and in small chunks. Other books aren't organized the same way, and this means you have to extrapolate how I've made you do this to how their content is organized. The best way to do this is to read the book lightly and make a list of all the major code sections. Turn this list into a set of exercises based on the chapters, and then simply do them in order one at a time.

The preceding process also works for new technologies, assuming they have books you can read. For anything without books, you do the above process but use online documentation or source code as your initial introduction.

Each new language you learn makes you a better programmer, and as you learn more languages they become easier to learn. By your third or fourth language you should be able to pick up similar languages in a week, with stranger languages taking longer. Now that you know Python you could potentially learn Ruby and JavaScript fairly quickly by comparison. This is simply because many languages share similar concepts, and once you learn the concepts in one language they work in others.

The final thing to remember about learning a new language is this: Don't be a stupid tourist. A stupid tourist is someone who goes to another country and then complains that the food isn't like the food at home ("Why can't I get a good burger in this stupid country?!"). When you're learning a new language, assume that what it does isn't stupid, it's just different, and embrace it so you can learn it.

After you learn a language, though, don't be a slave to that language's way of doing things. Sometimes the people who use a language actually do some very idiotic things for no other reason than "that's how we've always done it." If you like your style better and you know how everyone else does it, then feel free to break their rules if it improves things.

I really enjoy learning new programming languages. I think of myself as a "programmer anthropologist" and think of languages as little insights about the group of programmers who use them. I'm learning a language they all use to talk to each other through computers, and I find this fascinating. Then again, I'm kind of a weird guy, so just learn programming languages because you want to.

Enjoy! This is really fun stuff.

Advice from an Old Programmer

You've finished this book and have decided to continue with programming. Maybe it will be a career for you, or maybe it will be a hobby. You'll need some advice to make sure you continue on the right path and get the most enjoyment out of your newly chosen activity.

I've been programming for a very long time. So long that it's incredibly boring to me. At the time that I wrote this book, I knew about 20 programming languages and could learn new ones in about a day to a week depending on how weird they were. Eventually, though, this just became boring and couldn't hold my interest anymore. This doesn't mean I think programming *is* boring, or that *you* will think it's boring, only that *I* find it uninteresting at this point in my journey.

What I discovered after this journey of learning is that it's not the languages that matter but what you do with them. Actually, I always knew that, but I'd get distracted by the languages and forget it periodically. Now I never forget it, and neither should you.

Which programming language you learn and use doesn't matter. Do *not* get sucked into the religion surrounding programming languages as that will only blind you to their true purpose of being your tool for doing interesting things.

Programming as an intellectual activity is the *only* art form that allows you to create interactive art. You can create projects that other people can play with, and you can talk to them indirectly. No other art form is quite this interactive. Movies flow to the audience in one direction. Paintings do not move. Code goes both ways.

Programming as a profession is only moderately interesting. It can be a good job, but you could make about the same money and be happier running a fast food joint. You're much better off using code as your secret weapon in another profession.

People who can code in the world of technology companies are a dime a dozen and get no respect. People who can code in biology, medicine, government, sociology, physics, history, and mathematics are respected and can do amazing things to advance those disciplines.

Of course, all of this advice is pointless. If you liked learning to write software with this book, you should try to use it to improve your life any way you can. Go out and explore this weird, wonderful, new intellectual pursuit that barely anyone in the last 50 years has been able to explore. Might as well enjoy it while you can.

Finally, I'll say that learning to create software changes you and makes you different. Not better or worse, just different. You may find that people treat you harshly because you can create software, maybe using words like "nerd." Maybe you'll find that because you can dissect their logic they hate arguing with you. You may even find that simply knowing how a computer works makes you annoying and weird to them.

To this I have just one piece of advice: they can go to hell. The world needs more weird people who know how things work and who love to figure it all out. When they treat you like this, just remember that this is *your* journey, not theirs. Being different is not a crime, and people who tell you it is are just jealous that you've picked up a skill they never in their wildest dreams could acquire.

You can code. They cannot. That is pretty damn cool.

Command Line Crash Course

This appendix is a super fast course in using the command line. It is intended to be done rapidly in about a day or two, and not meant to teach you advanced shell usage.

Introduction: Shut Up and Shell

This appendix is a crash course in using the command line to make your computer perform tasks. As a crash course, it's not as detailed or extensive as my other books. It is simply designed to get you barely capable enough to start using your computer like a real programmer does. When you're done with this appendix, you will be able to give most of the basic commands that every shell user touches every day. You'll understand the basics of directories and a few other concepts.

The only piece of advice I am going to give you is this:

> *Shut up and type all of this in.*

Sorry to be mean, but that's what you have to do. If you have an irrational fear of the command line, the only way to conquer an irrational fear is to just shut up and fight through it.

You are not going to destroy your computer. You are not going to be thrown into some jail at the bottom of Microsoft's Redmond campus. Your friends won't laugh at you for being a nerd. Simply ignore any stupid weird reasons you have for fearing the command line.

Why? Because if you want to learn to code, then you must learn this. Programming languages are advanced ways to control your computer with language. The command line is the baby brother of programming languages. Learning the command line teaches you to control the computer using language. Once you get past that, you can then move on to writing code and feeling like you actually own the hunk of metal you just bought.

How to Use This Appendix

The best way to use this appendix is to do the following:

- Get yourself a small paper notebook and a pen.
- Start at the beginning of the appendix and do each exercise exactly as you're told.
- When you read something that doesn't make sense or that you don't understand, *write it down in your notebook*. Leave a little space so you can write an answer.

- After you finish an exercise, go back through your notebook and review the questions you have. Try to answer them by searching online and asking friends who might know the answer. Email me at help@learncodethehardway.org and I'll help you too.

Just keep going through this process of doing an exercise, writing down questions you have, then going back through and answering the questions you can. By the time you're done, you'll actually know a lot more than you think about using the command line.

You Will Be Memorizing Things

I'm warning you ahead of time that I'm going to make you memorize things right away. This is the quickest way to get you capable at something, but for some people memorization is painful. Just fight through it and do it anyway. Memorization is an important skill in learning things, so you should get over your fear of it.

Here's how you memorize things:

- Tell yourself you *will* do it. Don't try to find tricks or easy ways out of it, just sit down and do it.

- Write what you want to memorize on some index cards. Put one half of what you need to learn on one side, then another half on the other side.

- Every day for about 15 to 30 minutes, drill yourself on the index cards, trying to recall each one. Put any cards you don't get right into a different pile, just drill those cards until you get bored, then try the whole deck and see if you improve.

- Before you go to bed, drill just the cards you got wrong for about 5 minutes, then go to sleep.

There are other techniques, like you can write what you need to learn on a sheet of paper, laminate it, then stick it to the wall of your shower. While you're bathing, drill the knowledge without looking, and when you get stuck glance at it to refresh your memory.

If you do this every day, you should be able to memorize most things I tell you to memorize in about a week to a month. Once you do, nearly everything else becomes easier and intuitive, which is the purpose of memorization. It's not to teach you abstract concepts but rather to ingrain the basics so that they are intuitive and you don't have to think about them. Once you've memorized these basics they stop being speed bumps preventing you from learning more advanced abstract concepts.

The Setup

In this appendix you will be instructed to do three things:

- Do some things in your shell (command line, Terminal, PowerShell).

- Learn about what you just did.

- Do more on your own.

For this first exercise you'll be expected to get your Terminal open and working so that you can do the rest of the appendix.

Do This

Get your Terminal, shell, or PowerShell working so you can access it quickly and know that it works.

macOS

For macOS you'll need to do this:

- Hold down the command key and hit the spacebar.
- A search bar will pop up.
- Type: Terminal
- Click on the Terminal application that looks kind of like a black box.
- This will open Terminal.
- You can now go to your dock and CTRL-click to pull up the menu, then select Options → Keep In dock.

Now you have your Terminal open, and it's in your dock so you can get to it.

Linux

I'm assuming that if you have Linux then you already know how to get at your Terminal. Look through the menu for your window manager for anything named "Shell" or "Terminal."

Windows

On Windows we're going to use PowerShell. People used to work with a program called cmd.exe, but it's not nearly as usable as PowerShell. If you have Windows 7 or later, do this:

- Click Start.
- In "Search programs and files" type "powershell."
- Hit Enter.

If you don't have Windows 7, you should *seriously* consider upgrading. If you still insist on not upgrading, then you can try installing PowerShell from Microsoft's download center. Search online to find "powershell downloads" for your version of Windows. You are on your own, though, since I don't have Windows XP, but hopefully the PowerShell experience is the same.

You Learned This

You learned how to get your Terminal open so you can do the rest of this appendix.

WARNING! If you have that really smart friend who already knows Linux, ignore her when she tells you to use something other than Bash. I'm teaching you Bash. That's it. She will claim that zsh will give you 30 more IQ points and win you millions in the stock market. Ignore her. Your goal is to get capable enough, and at this level it doesn't matter which shell you use. The next warning is stay off IRC or other places where "hackers" hang out. They think it's funny to hand you commands that can destroy your computer. The command `rm -rf /` is a classic that you *must never type*. Just avoid them. If you need help, make sure you get it from someone you trust and not from random idiots on the internet.

Do More

This exercise has a large "do more" part. The other exercises are not as involved as this one, but I'm having you prime your brain for the rest of the appendix by doing some memorization. Just trust me: this will make things silky smooth later on.

Linux/macOS

Take this list of commands and create index cards with the names on the left on one side, and the definitions on the other side. Drill them every day while continuing with the lessons in this appendix.

pwd   print working directory

hostname   my computer's network name

mkdir   make directory

cd   change directory

ls   list directory

rmdir   remove directory

pushd   push directory

popd   pop directory

cp   copy a file or directory

mv   move a file or directory

less   page through a file

cat   print the whole file

xargs   execute arguments

find   find files

grep   find things inside files

man   read a manual page

apropos   find which manual page is appropriate

env   look at your environment

echo   print some arguments

export   export/set a new environment variable

exit   exit the shell

sudo   DANGER! become super user root DANGER!

Windows

If you're using Windows then here's your list of commands:

pwd   print working directory

hostname   my computer's network name

mkdir   make directory

cd   change directory

ls   list directory

rmdir   remove directory

pushd   push directory

popd   pop directory

cp   copy a file or directory

robocopy   robust copy

mv   move a file or directory

more   page through a file

type   print the whole file

forfiles   run a command on lots of files

dir -r   find files

select-string   find things inside files

help   read a manual page

helpctr   find what manual page is appropriate

echo   print some arguments

set   export/set a new environment variable

exit   exit the shell

runas   DANGER! become super user root DANGER!

Drill, drill, drill! Drill until you can say these phrases right away when you see that word. Then drill the inverse, so that you read the phrase and know what command will do that. You're building your vocabulary by doing this, but don't spend so much time you go nuts and get bored.

Paths, Folders, Directories (pwd)

In this exercise you learn how to print your working directory with the pwd command.

Do This

I'm going to teach you how to read these "sessions" that I show you. You don't have to type everything I list here, just some of the parts:

- You do *not* type in the $ (Unix) or > (Windows). That's just me showing you my session so you can see what I got.

- You type in the stuff after $ or >, then hit Enter. So if I have $ pwd, you type just pwd and hit Enter.

- You can then see what I have for output followed by another $ or > prompt. That content is the output, and you should see the same output.

Let's do a simple first command so you can get the hang of this:

Linux/macOS

Exercise 2 Session
```
$ pwd
/Users/zedshaw
$
```

Windows

```
PS C:\Users\zed> pwd

Path
----
C:\Users\zed

PS C:\Users\zed>
```

WARNING! In this appendix I need to save space so that you can focus on the important details of the commands. To do this, I'm going to strip out the first part of the prompt (the PS C:\Users\zed above) and leave just the little > part. This means your prompt won't look exactly the same, but don't worry about that. Remember that from now on I'll only have the > to tell you that's the prompt. I'm doing the same thing for the Unix prompts, but Unix prompts are so varied that most people get used to $ meaning "just the prompt."

You Learned This

Your prompt will look different from mine. You may have your user name before the $ and the name of your computer. On Windows it will probably look different too. The key is that you see the following pattern:

- There's a prompt.
- You type a command there. In this case, it's pwd.
- It printed something.
- Repeat.

You just learned what pwd does, which means "print working directory." What's a directory? It's a folder. Folder and directory are the same thing, and they're used interchangeably. When you open your file browser on your computer to graphically find files, you are walking through folders. Those folders are the exact same things as these "directories" we're going to work with.

Do More

- Type pwd 20 times and each time say "print working directory."

- Write down the path that this command gives you. Find it with your graphical file browser of choice.

- No, seriously, type it 20 times and say it out loud. Sssh. Just do it.

If You Get Lost

As you go through these instructions you may get lost. You may not know where you are or where a file is and have no idea how to continue. To solve this problem I am going to teach you the commands to type to stop being lost.

Whenever you get lost, it is most likely because you were typing commands and have no idea where you've ended up. What you should do is type pwd to *print your current directory*. This tells you where you are.

The next thing is you need to have a way of getting back to where you are safe, your home. To do this type cd ~ and you are back in your home.

This means if you get lost at any time type:

```
pwd
cd ~
```

The first command pwd tells you where you are. The second command cd ~ takes you home so you can try again.

Do This

Right now figure out where you are, and then go home using pwd and cd ~. This will make sure you are always in the right place.

You Learned This

How to get back to your home if you ever get lost.

Make a Directory (`mkdir`)

In this exercise you learn how to make a new directory (folder) using the `mkdir` command.

Do This

Remember! *You need to go home first!* Do your pwd then cd ~ before doing this exercise. Before you do *all* exercises in this appendix, always go home first!

Linux/macOS

```
$ pwd
$ cd ~
$ mkdir temp
$ mkdir temp/stuff
$ mkdir temp/stuff/things
$ mkdir -p temp/stuff/things/orange/apple/pear/grape
$
```

Windows

```
> pwd
> cd ~
> mkdir temp


    Directory: C:\Users\zed


Mode                LastWriteTime     Length Name
----                -------------     ------ ----
d----         12/17/2011   9:02 AM           temp


> mkdir temp/stuff


    Directory: C:\Users\zed\temp


Mode                LastWriteTime     Length Name
----                -------------     ------ ----
d----         12/17/2011   9:02 AM           stuff


> mkdir temp/stuff/things


    Directory: C:\Users\zed\temp\stuff

Mode                LastWriteTime     Length Name
----                -------------     ------ ----
d----         12/17/2011   9:03 AM           things


> mkdir temp/stuff/things/orange/apple/pear/grape
```

```
Directory: C:\Users\zed\temp\stuff\things\orange\apple\pear


Mode                 LastWriteTime        Length Name
----                 -------------        ------ ----
d----        12/17/2011   9:03 AM                grape


>
```

This is the only time I'll list the pwd and cd ~ commands. They are expected in the exercises *every time*. Do them all the time.

You Learned This

Now we get into typing more than one command. These are all the different ways you can run mkdir. What does mkdir do? It makes directories. Why are you asking that? You should be doing your index cards and getting your commands memorized. If you don't know that "mkdir makes directories" then keep working the index cards.

What does it mean to make a directory? You might call directories "folders." They're the same thing. All you did above is create directories inside directories inside of more directories. This is called a "path" and it's a way of saying "first temp, then stuff, then things, and that's where I want it." It's a set of directions to the computer of where you want to put something in the tree of folders (directories) that make up your computer's hard disk.

WARNING! In this appendix I'm using the / (slash) character for all paths since they work the same on all computers now. However, Windows users will need to know that you can also use the \ (backslash) character and other Windows users will typically expect that at times.

Do More

- The concept of a "path" might confuse you at this point. Don't worry. We'll do a lot more with them, and then you'll get it.

- Make 20 other directories inside the temp directory in various levels. Go look at them with a graphical file browser.

- Make a directory with a space in the name by putting quotes around it: mkdir "I Have Fun"

- If the temp directory already exists then you'll get an error. Use cd to change to a work directory that you can control and try it there. On Windows, Desktop is a good place.

Change Directory (cd)

In this exercise you learn how to change from one cirectory to another using the cd command.

Do This

I'm going to give you the instructions for these sessions one more time:

- You do *not* type in the $ (Unix) or > (Windows).
- You type in the stuff after this, then hit Enter. If I have $ cd terrp, you just type cd temp and hit Enter.
- The output comes after you hit Enter, followed by another $ or > prompt.
- Always go home first! Do pwd and then cd ~, so you go back to your starting point.

Linux/macOS

```
$ cd temp
$ pwd
~/temp
$ cd stuff
$ pwd
~/temp/stuff
$ cd things
$ pwd
~/temp/stuff/things
$ cd orange/
$ pwd
~/temp/stuff/things/orange
$ cd apple/
$ pwd
~/temp/stuff/things/orange/apple
$ cd pear/
$ pwd
~/temp/stuff/things/orange/apple/pear
$ cd grape/
$ pwd
~/temp/stuff/things/orange/apple/pear/grape
$ cd ..
$ cd ..
$ pwd
~/temp/stuff/things/orange/apple
$ cd ..
$ cd ..
$ pwd
```

```
~/temp/stuff/things
$ cd ../../..
$ pwd
~/
$ cd temp/stuff/things/orange/apple/pear/grape
$ pwd
~/temp/stuff/things/orange/apple/pear/grape
$ cd ../../../../../../../
$ pwd
~/
$
```

Windows

```
> cd temp
> pwd

Path
----
C:\Users\zed\temp


> cd stuff
> pwd

Path
----
C:\Users\zed\temp\stuff


> cd things
> pwd

Path
----
C:\Users\zed\temp\stuff\things


> cd orange
> pwd

Path
----
C:\Users\zed\temp\stuff\things\orange


> cd apple
> pwd
```

```
Path
----
C:\Users\zed\temp\stuff\things\orange\apple


> cd pear
> pwd

Path
----
C:\Users\zed\temp\stuff\things\orange\apple\pear


> cd grape
> pwd

Path
----
C:\Users\zed\temp\stuff\things\orange\apple\pear\grape


> cd ..
> cd ..
> cd ..
> pwd

Path
----
C:\Users\zed\temp\stuff\things\orange


> cd ../..
> pwd

Path
----
C:\Users\zed\temp\stuff


> cd ..
> cd ..
> cd temp/stuff/things/orange/apple/pear/grape
> cd ../../../../../../
> pwd

Path
----
C:\Users\zed


>
```

You Learned This

You made all these directories in the last exercise, and now you're just moving around inside them with the `cd` command. In my session above I also use pwd to check where I am, so remember not to type the output that pwd prints. For example, on line 3 you see ~/temp, but that's the output of pwd from the prompt above it. *Do not type this in.*

You should also see how I use the `..` to move "up" in the tree and path.

Do More

A very important part of learning to use the command line interface (CLI) on a computer with a graphical user interface (GUI) is figuring out how they work together. When I started using computers there was no GUI, and you did everything with the DOS prompt (the CLI). Later, when computers became powerful enough that everyone could have graphics, it was simple for me to match CLI directories with GUI windows and folders.

Most people today, however, have no comprehension of the CLI, paths, and directories. In fact, it's very difficult to teach it to them, and the only way to learn about the connection is for you to constantly work with the CLI until one day it clicks that things you do in the GUI will show up in the CLI.

The way you do this is by spending some time finding directories with your GUI file browser, then going to them with your CLI. This is what you'll do next.

- `cd` to the `apple` directory with one command.
- `cd` back to `temp` with one command, but not further above that.
- Find out how to `cd` to your "home directory" with one command.
- `cd` to your Documents directory, then find it with your GUI file browser (Finder, Windows Explorer, etc.).
- `cd` to your Downloads directory, then find it with your file browser.
- Find another directory with your file browser, then `cd` to it.
- Remember when you put quotes around a directory with spaces in it? You can do that with any command. For example, if you have a directory I Have Fun, then you can do: `cd "I Have Fun"`.

List Directory (`ls`)

In this exercise you learn how to list the contents of a directory with the `ls` command.

Do This

Before you start, make sure you `cd` back to the directory above `temp`. If you have no idea where you are, use pwd to figure it out and then move there.

Linux/macOS

```
$ cd temp
$ ls
stuff
$ cd stuff
$ ls
things
$ cd things
$ ls
orange
$ cd orange
$ ls
apple
$ cd apple
$ ls
pear
$ cd pear
$ ls
$ cd grape
$ ls
$ cd ..
$ ls
grape
$ cd ../../../
$ ls
orange
$ cd ../../
$ ls
stuff
$
```

Windows

```
> cd temp
> ls


    Directory: C:\Users\zed\temp


Mode                 LastWriteTime         Length Name
----                 -------------         ------ ----
d----        12/17/2011   9:03 AM                stuff
```

```
> cd stuff
> ls


    Directory: C:\Users\zed\temp\stuff


Mode                LastWriteTime        Length Name
----                -------------        ------ ----
d----         12/17/2011   9:03 AM              things


> cd things
> ls


    Directory: C:\Users\zed\temp\stuff\things


Mode                LastWriteTime        Length Name
----                -------------        ------ ----
d----         12/17/2011   9:03 AM              orange


> cd orange
> ls


    Directory: C:\Users\zed\temp\stuff\things\orange


Mode                LastWriteTime        Length Name
----                -------------        ------ ----
d----         12/17/2011   9:03 AM              apple


> cd apple
> ls


    Directory: C:\Users\zed\temp\stuff\things\orange\apple


Mode                LastWriteTime        Length Name
----                -------------        ------ ----
d----         12/17/2011   9:03 AM              pear


> cd pear
> ls
```

```
    Directory: C:\Users\zed\temp\stuff\things\orange\apple\pear


Mode                LastWriteTime     Length Name
----                -------------     ------ ----
d----         12/17/2011   9:03 AM           grape


> cd grape
> ls
> cd ..
> ls


    Directory: C:\Users\zed\temp\stuff\things\orange\apple\pear


Mode                LastWriteTime     Length Name
----                -------------     ------ ----
d----         12/17/2011   9:03 AM           grape


> cd ..
> ls


    Directory: C:\Users\zed\temp\stuff\things\orange\apple


Mode                LastWriteTime     Length Name
----                -------------     ------ ----
d----         12/17/2011   9:03 AM           pear


> cd ../../..
> ls


    Directory: C:\Users\zed\temp\stuff


Mode                LastWriteTime     Length Name
----                -------------     ------ ----
d----         12/17/2011   9:03 AM           things


> cd ..
> ls
```

```
Directory: C:\Users\zed\temp


Mode                LastWriteTime       Length Name
----                -------------       ------ ----
d----         12/17/2011    9:03 AM            stuff


>
```

You Learned This

The `ls` command lists out the contents of the directory you are currently in. You can see me use `cd` to change into different directories and then list what's in them so I know which directory to go to next.

There are a lot of options for the `ls` command, but you'll learn how to get help on those later when we cover the `help` command.

Do More

- *Type every one of these commands in!* You have to actually type these to learn them. Just reading them is *not* good enough. I'll stop yelling now.
- On Unix, try the `ls -lR` command while you're in `temp`.
- On Windows do the same thing with `dir -R`.
- Use `cd` to get to other directories on your computer, and then use `ls` to see what's in them.
- Update your notebook with new questions. I know you probably have some, because I'm not covering everything about this command.
- Remember that if you get lost, use `ls` and `pwd` to figure out where you are, and then go to where you need to be with `cd`.

Remove Directory (`rmdir`)

In this exercise you learn how to remove an empty directory.

Do This

Linux/macOS

```
$ cd temp
$ ls
stuff
$ cd stuff/things/orange/apple/pear/grape/
$ cd ..
$ rmdir grape
$ cd ..
$ rmdir pear
$ cd ..
$ ls
apple
$ rmdir apple
$ cd ..
$ ls
orange
$ rmdir orange
$ cd ..
$ ls
things
$ rmdir things
$ cd ..
$ ls
stuff
$ rmdir stuff
$ pwd
~/temp
$
```

WARNING! If you try to do `rmdir` on macOS and it refuses to remove the directory even though you are *positive* it's empty, then there is actually a file in there called `.DS_Store`. In that case, type `rm -rf <dir>` instead (replace `<dir>` with the directory name).

Windows

```
> cd temp
> ls

    Directory: C:\Users\zed\temp
```

Mode	LastWriteTime	Length	Name
d----	12/17/2011 9:03 AM		stuff

```
> cd stuff/things/orange/apple/pear/grape/
> cd ..
> rmdir grape
> cd ..
> rmdir pear
> cd ..
> rmdir apple
> cd ..
> rmdir orange
> cd ..
> ls
```

    Directory: C:\Users\zed\temp\stuff

Mode	LastWriteTime	Length	Name
d----	12/17/2011 9:14 AM		things

```
> rmdir things
> cd ..
> ls
```

    Directory: C:\Users\zed\temp

Mode	LastWriteTime	Length	Name
d----	12/17/2011 9:14 AM		stuff

```
> rmdir stuff
> pwd
```

```
Path
----
C:\Users\zed\temp
```

```
> cd ..
>
```

You Learned This

I'm now mixing up the commands, so make sure you type them exactly and pay attention. Every time you make a mistake, it's because you aren't paying attention. If you find yourself making many mistakes, then take a break or just quit for the day. You've always got tomorrow to try again.

In this example you'll learn how to remove a directory. It's easy. You just go to the directory right above it, then type `rmdir <dir>`, replacing `<dir>` with the name of the directory to remove.

Do More

- Make 20 more directories and remove them all.
- Make a single path of directories that is 10 deep and remove them one at a time just like I did previously.
- If you try to remove a directory with contents, you will get an error. I'll show you how to remove those in later exercises.

Moving Around (`pushd`, `popd`)

In this exercise you learn how to save your current location and go to a new location with `pushd`. You then learn how to return to the saved location with `popd`.

Do This

Linux/macOS

Exercise 8 Session

```
$ cd temp
$ mkdir i/like/icecream
$ pushd i/like/icecream
~/temp/i/like/icecream ~/temp
$ popd
~/temp
$ pwd
~/temp
$ pushd i/like
~/temp/i/like ~/temp
$ pwd
~/temp/i/like
$ pushd icecream
~/temp/i/like/icecream ~/temp/i/like ~/temp
$ pwd
```

```
~/temp/i/like/icecream
$ popd
~/temp/i/like ~/temp
$ pwd
~/temp/i/like
$ popd
~/temp
$ pushd i/like/icecream
~/temp/i/like/icecream ~/temp
$ pushd
~/temp ~/temp/i/like/icecream
$ pwd
~/temp
$ pushd
~/temp/i/like/icecream ~/temp
$ pwd
~/temp/i/like/icecream
$
```

Windows

```
> cd temp
> mkdir i/like/icecream


    Directory: C:\Users\zed\temp\i\like


Mode                LastWriteTime     Length Name
----                -------------     ------ ----
d----         12/20/2011  11:05 AM           icecream


> pushd i/like/icecream
> popd
> pwd

Path
----
C:\Users\zed\temp


> pushd i/like
> pwd

Path
----
C:\Users\zed\temp\i\like
```

```
> pushd icecream
> pwd

Path
----
C:\Users\zed\temp\i\like\icecream


> popd
> pwd

Path
----
C:\Users\zed\temp\i\like


> popd
>
```

WARNING! In Windows you normally don't need the -p option like you do in Linux. *However*, I believe this is a more recent development, so you may run into older Windows PowerShell versions that do require the -p. If you have more information on this please email me at help@learncodethehardway.org, so I can sort out whether to mention -p for Windows or not.

You Learned This

You're getting into programmer territory with these commands, but they're so handy I have to teach them to you. These commands let you temporarily go to a different directory and then come back, easily switching between the two.

The pushd command takes your current directory and "pushes" it into a list for later, then it *changes* to another directory. It's like saying, "Save where I am, then go here."

The popd command takes the last directory you pushed and "pops" it off, taking you back there.

Finally, on Unix pushd, if you run it by itself with no arguments, it will switch between your current directory and the last one you pushed. It's an easy way to switch between two directories. *This does not work in PowerShell.*

Do More

* Use these commands to move around directories all over your computer.
* Remove the i/like/icecream directories and make your own, then move around in them.

- Explain to yourself the output that `pushd` and `popd` will print out for you. Notice how it works like a stack?

- You already know this, but remember that `mkdir -p` (on Linux/macOS) will make an entire path even if all the directories don't exist. That's what I did first for this exercise.

- Remember that Windows will make a full path and does not need the `-p`.

Making Empty Files (`touch/New-Item`)

In this exercise you learn how to make an empty file using the `touch` (`New-Item` on Windows) command.

Do This

Linux/macOS

Exercise 9 Session

```
$ cd temp
$ touch iamcool.txt
$ ls
iamcool.txt
$
```

Windows

Exercise 9 Windows Session

```
> cd temp
> New-Item iamcool.txt -type file
> ls


        Directory: C:\Users\zed\temp


Mode                LastWriteTime     Length Name
----                -------------     ------ ----
-a---        12/17/2011    9:03 AM            iamcool.txt


>
```

You Learned This

You learned how to make an empty file. On Unix `touch` does this, and it also changes the times on the file. I rarely use it for anything other than making empty files. On Windows you don't have this command, so you learned how to use the `New-Item` command, which does the same thing but can also make new directories.

Do More

- Unix: Make a directory, change to it, and then make a file in it. Then change one level up and run the rmdir command in this directory. You *should* get an error. Try to understand why you got this error.

- Windows: Do the same thing, but you won't get an error. You'll get a prompt asking if you really want to remove the directory.

Copy a File (cp)

In this exercise you learn how to copy a file from one location to another with the cp command.

Do This

Linux/macOS

Exercise 10 Session

```
$ cd temp
$ cp iamcool.txt neat.txt
$ ls
iamcool.txt neat.txt
$ cp neat.txt awesome.txt
$ ls
awesome.txt iamcool.txt neat.txt
$ cp awesome.txt thefourthfile.txt
$ ls
awesome.txt  iamcool.txt  neat.txt  thefourthfile.txt
$ mkdir something
$ cp awesome.txt something/
$ ls
awesome.txt iamcool.txt  neat.txt  something  thefourthfile.txt
$ ls something/
awesome.txt
$ cp -r something newplace
$ ls newplace/
awesome.txt
$
```

Windows

Exercise 10 Windows Session

```
> cd temp
> cp iamcool.txt neat.txt
> ls
```

```
    Directory: C:\Users\zed\temp


Mode                LastWriteTime      Length Name
----                -------------      ------ ----
-a---       12/22/2011    4:49 PM           0 iamcool.txt
-a---       12/22/2011    4:49 PM           0 neat.txt


> cp neat.txt awesome.txt
> ls


    Directory: C:\Users\zed\temp


Mode                LastWriteTime      Length Name
----                -------------      ------ ----
-a---       12/22/2011    4:49 PM           0 awesome.txt
-a---       12/22/2011    4:49 PM           0 iamcool.txt
-a---       12/22/2011    4:49 PM           0 neat.txt


> cp awesome.txt thefourthfile.txt
> ls


    Directory: C:\Users\zed\temp


Mode                LastWriteTime      Length Name
----                -------------      ------ ----
-a---       12/22/2011    4:49 PM           0 awesome.txt
-a---       12/22/2011    4:49 PM           0 iamcool.txt
-a---       12/22/2011    4:49 PM           0 neat.txt
-a---       12/22/2011    4:49 PM           0 thefourthfile.txt


> mkdir something


    Directory: C:\Users\zed\temp


Mode                LastWriteTime      Length Name
----                -------------      ------ ----
d----       12/22/2011    4:52 PM             something


> cp awesome.txt something/
```

```
> ls

    Directory: C:\Users\zed\temp

Mode                LastWriteTime        Length Name
----                -------------        ------ ----
d----       12/22/2011    4:52 PM               something
-a---       12/22/2011    4:49 PM             0 awesome.txt
-a---       12/22/2011    4:49 PM             0 iamcool.txt
-a---       12/22/2011    4:49 PM             0 neat.txt
-a---       12/22/2011    4:49 PM             0 thefourthfile.txt


> ls something

    Directory: C:\Users\zed\temp\something


Mode                LastWriteTime        Length Name
----                -------------        ------ ----
-a---       12/22/2011    4:49 PM             0 awesome.txt


> cp -recurse something newplace
> ls newplace

    Directory: C:\Users\zed\temp\newplace


Mode                LastWriteTime        Length Name
----                -------------        ------ ----
-a---       12/22/2011    4:49 PM             0 awesome.txt

>
```

You Learned This

Now you can copy files. It's simple to just take a file and copy it to a new one. In this exercise I also make a new directory and copy a file into that directory.

I'm going to tell you a secret about programmers and system administrators now. They are lazy. I'm lazy. My friends are lazy. That's why we use computers. We like to make computers do boring things for us. In the exercises so far you have been typing repetitive boring commands so that you can learn them, but usually it's not like this. Usually, if you find yourself doing something boring and repetitive there's probably a programmer who has figured out how to make it easier. You just don't know about it yet.

The other thing about programmers is they aren't nearly as clever as you think. If you overthink what to type, then you'll probably get it wrong. Instead, try to imagine what the name of a command is to you and try it. Chances are that it's a name or some abbreviation similar to what you thought it was. If you still can't figure it out intuitively, then ask around and search online. Hopefully, it's not something really stupid like ROBOCOPY.

Do More

- Use the `cp -r` command to copy more directories with files in them.
- Copy a file to your home directory or desktop.
- Find these files in your GUI and open them in a text editor.
- Notice how sometimes I put a / (slash) at the end of a directory? That makes sure the file is really a directory, so if the directory doesn't exist I'll get an error.

Moving a File (mv)

In this exercise you learn how to move a file from one location to another using the mv command.

Do This

Linux/macOS

```
$ cd temp
$ mv awesome.txt uncool.txt
$ ls
newplace  uncool.txt
$ mv newplace oldplace
$ ls
oldplace  uncool.txt
$ mv oldplace newplace
$ ls
newplace  uncool.txt
$
```

Windows

```
> cd temp
> mv awesome.txt uncool.txt
> ls
```

```
    Directory: C:\Users\zed\temp


Mode                LastWriteTime     Length Name
----                -------------     ------ ----
d----        12/22/2011   4:52 PM            newplace
d----        12/22/2011   4:52 PM            something
-a---        12/22/2011   4:49 PM          0 iamcool.txt
-a---        12/22/2011   4:49 PM          0 neat.txt
-a---        12/22/2011   4:49 PM          0 thefourthfile.txt
-a---        12/22/2011   4:49 PM          0 uncool.txt


> mv newplace oldplace
> ls


    Directory: C:\Users\zed\temp


Mode                LastWriteTime     Length Name
----                -------------     ------ ----
d----        12/22/2011   4:52 PM            oldplace
d----        12/22/2011   4:52 PM            something
-a---        12/22/2011   4:49 PM          0 iamcool.txt
-a---        12/22/2011   4:49 PM          0 neat.txt
-a---        12/22/2011   4:49 PM          0 thefourthfile.txt
-a---        12/22/2011   4:49 PM          0 uncool.txt


> mv oldplace newplace
> ls newplace


    Directory: C:\Users\zed\temp\newplace


Mode                LastWriteTime     Length Name
----                -------------     ------ ----
-a---        12/22/2011   4:49 PM          0 awesome.txt


> ls


    Directory: C:\Users\zed\temp


Mode                LastWriteTime     Length Name
----                -------------     ------ ----
```

```
d----        12/22/2011    4:52 PM              newplace
d----        12/22/2011    4:52 PM              something
-a---        12/22/2011    4:49 PM          0   iamcool.txt
-a---        12/22/2011    4:49 PM          0   neat.txt
-a---        12/22/2011    4:49 PM          0   thefourthfile.txt
-a---        12/22/2011    4:49 PM          0   uncool.txt


>
```

You Learned This

Moving files or, rather, renaming them. It's easy: give the old name and the new name.

Do More

Move a file in the `newplace` directory to another directory, then move it back.

View a File (`less`/`more`)

To do this exercise you're going to do some work using the commands you know so far. You'll also need a text editor that can make plain text (.txt) files. Here's what you do:

- Open your text editor and type some stuff into a new file. On macOS this could be TextWrangler. On Windows this might be Notepad++. On Linux this could be gedit. Any editor will work.

- Save that file to your desktop and name it `test.txt`.

- In your shell use the commands you know to *copy* this file to your `temp` directory that you've been working with.

Once you've done that, complete this exercise.

Do This

Linux/macOS

Exercise 12 Session

```
$ less test.txt
[displays file here]
$
```

That's it. To get out of less just type q (as in quit).

Windows

```
> more test.txt
[displays file here]
>
```

WARNING! In the preceding output I'm showing [displays file here] to "abbreviate" what that program shows. I'll do this when I mean to say, "Showing you the output of this program is too complex, so just insert what you see on your computer here and pretend I did show it to you." Your screen will not actually show this.

You Learned This

This is one way to look at the contents of a file. It's useful because if the file has many lines, it will "page" so that only one screenful at a time is visible. In the *Do More* section you'll play with this some more.

Do More

- Open your text file again and repeatedly copy-paste the text so that it's about 50–100 lines long.

- Copy it to your temp directory again so you can look at it.

- Now do the exercise again, but this time page through it. On Unix you use the spacebar and w (the letter *w*) to go down and up. Arrow keys also work. On Windows just hit the spacebar to page through.

- Look at some of the empty files you created, too.

- The cp command will overwrite files that already exist, so be careful copying files around.

Stream a File (cat)

You're going to do some more setup for this one so you get used to making files in one program and then accessing them from the command line. With the same text editor from the last exercise, create another file named test2.txt, but this time save it directly to your temp directory.

Do This

Linux/macOS

```
$ less test2.txt
[displays file here]
$ cat test2.txt
I am a fun guy.
Don't you know why?
Because I make poems,
that make babies cry.
$ cat test.txt
Hi there this is cool.
$
```

Windows

```
> more test2.txt
[displays file here]
> cat test2.txt
I am a fun guy.
Don't you know why?
Because I make poems,
that make babies cry.
> cat test.txt
Hi there this is cool.
>
```

Remember that when I say [displays file here] I'm abbreviating the output of that command so I don't have to show you exactly everything.

You Learned This

Do you like my poem? Totally going to win a Nobel. Anyway, you already know the first command, and I'm just having you check that your file is there. Then you cat the file to the screen. This command just spews the whole file to the screen with no paging or stopping. To demonstrate that, I have you do this to test.txt, which should just spew a bunch of lines from that exercise.

Do More

- Make a few more text files and work with cat.
- Unix: Try cat test.txt test2.txt, and see what it does.
- Windows: Try cat test.txt,test2.txt, and see what it does.

Removing a File (rm)

In this exercise you learn how to remove (delete) a file using the rm command.

Do This

Linux

```
$ cd temp
$ ls
uncool.txt  iamcool.txt  neat.txt  something  thefourthfile.txt
$ rm uncool.txt
$ ls
iamcool.txt  neat.txt  something  thefourthfile.txt
$ rm iamcool.txt neat.txt thefourthfile.txt
$ ls
something
$ cp -r something newplace
$
$ rm something/awesome.txt
$ rmdir something
$ rm -rf newplace
$ ls
$
```

Windows

```
> cd temp
> ls


    Directory: C:\Users\zed\temp


Mode                LastWriteTime     Length Name
----                -------------     ------ ----
d----         12/22/2011   4:52 PM           newplace
d----         12/22/2011   4:52 PM           something
-a---         12/22/2011   4:49 PM        0  iamcool.txt
-a---         12/22/2011   4:49 PM        0  neat.txt
-a---         12/22/2011   4:49 PM        0  thefourthfile.txt
-a---         12/22/2011   4:49 PM        0  uncool.txt


> rm uncool.txt
> ls
```

```
    Directory: C:\Users\zed\temp


Mode                 LastWriteTime     Length Name
----                 -------------     ------ ----
d----        12/22/2011    4:52 PM            newplace
d----        12/22/2011    4:52 PM            something
-a---        12/22/2011    4:49 PM          0 iamcool.txt
-a---        12/22/2011    4:49 PM          0 neat.txt
-a---        12/22/2011    4:49 PM          0 thefourthfile.txt


> rm iamcool.txt
> rm neat.txt
> rm thefourthfile.txt
> ls


    Directory: C:\Users\zed\temp


Mode                 LastWriteTime     Length Name
----                 -------------     ------ ----
d----        12/22/2011    4:52 PM            newplace
d----        12/22/2011    4:52 PM            something


> cp -r something newplace
> rm something/awesome.txt
> rmdir something
> rm -r newplace
> ls
>
```

You Learned This

Here we clean up the files from the last exercise. Remember when I had you try to rmdir on a directory with something in it? Well, that failed because you can't remove a directory with files in it. To do that you have to remove the file or recursively delete all of its contents. That's what you did at the end of this.

Do More

- Clean up everything in temp from all the exercises so far.
- Write in your notebook to be careful when running recursive remove on files.

Exiting Your Terminal (exit)

Do This

Linux/macOS

Exercise 23 Session

```
$ exit
```

Windows

Exercise 23 Windows Session

```
> exit
```

You Learned This

Your final exercise is how to exit a Terminal. Again this is very easy, but I'm going to have you do more.

Do More

For your last set of exercises I'm going to have you use the help system to look up a set of commands you should research and learn how to use on your own.

Here's the list for Unix:

- xargs
- sudo
- chmod
- chown

For Windows look up these things:

- forfiles
- runas
- attrib
- icacls

Find out what these are, play with them, and then add them to your index cards.

Command Line Next Steps

You have completed the crash course. At this point you should be a barely capable shell user. There's a whole huge list of tricks and key sequences you don't know yet, and I'm going to give you a few final places to go research more.

Unix Bash References

The shell you've been using is called Bash. It's not the greatest shell, but it's everywhere and has a lot of features, so it's a good start. Here's a short list of links about Bash you should go read:

Bash Cheat Sheet   https://learncodethehardway.org/unix/bash_cheat_sheet.pdf   (created   by Raphael and CC licensed)

Reference Manual   http://www.gnu.org/software/bash/manual/bashref.html

PowerShell References

On Windows there's really only PowerShell. Here's a list of useful links for you related to PowerShell:

Owner's Manual   http://technet.microsoft.com/en-us/library/ee221100.aspx

Cheat Sheet   https://download.microsoft.com/download/2/1/2/2122F0B9-0EE6-4E6D-BFD6-F9DCD27C07F9/WS12_QuickRef_Download_Files/PowerShell_LangRef_v3.pdf

Master PowerShell   http://powershell.com/cs/blogs/ebook/default.aspx

Index

Register Your Product at informit.com/register

Access additional benefits and **save 35%** on your next purchase

- Automatically receive a coupon for 35% off your next purchase, valid for 30 days. Look for your code in your InformIT cart or the Manage Codes section of your account page.
- Download available product updates.
- Access bonus material if available.
- Check the box to hear from us and receive exclusive offers on new editions and related products.

InformIT.com—The Trusted Technology Learning Source

InformIT is the online home of information technology brands at Pearson, the world's foremost education company. At InformIT.com, you can:

- Shop our books, eBooks, software, and video training
- Take advantage of our special offers and promotions (informit.com/promotions)
- Sign up for special offers and content newsletter (informit.com/newsletters)
- Access thousands of free chapters and video lessons

Connect with InformIT—Visit informit.com/community

the trusted technology learning source

Addison-Wesley · Adobe Press · Cisco Press · Microsoft Press · Pearson IT Certification · Prentice Hall · Que · Sams · Peachpit Press

 Pearson